MAXIM G

Philistines

in a new version by
Andrew Upton

faber and faber

First published in 2007
by Faber and Faber Limited
3 Queen Square, London WC1N 3AU

Typeset by Country Setting, Kingsdown, Kent CT14 8ES
Printed in the UK by CPI Bookmarque, Croydon, CR0 4TD

A CIP record for this book
is available from the British Library

ISBN 978–0–571–23867–5

2 4 6 8 10 9 7 5 3 1

For Howard

An adaptation is the way it is
– is even there at all –
because of its production

Philistines in this version was first performed in the Lyttelton auditorium of the National Theatre, London, on 23 May 2007. The cast was as follows:

Vassilly Phil Davis
Akulina Stephanie Jacob
Tanya Ruth Wilson
Pyotr Rory Kinnear
Nil Mark Bonnar
Polya Susannah Fielding
Stepanida Maggie McCarthy
Perchikin Duncan Bell
Teterev Conleth Hill
Elena Justine Mitchell
Shyshkin Jonathan Bryan
Tsvetaeva Rendah Heywood
Doctor Marcus Cunningham
Old Crone Julia West
Old Man Mike Aherne
Ensemble Saskia Butler, Danny Nutt, Charlotte Pyke

Director Howard Davies
Designer Bunny Christie
Lighting Designer Neil Austin
Music Dominic Muldowney
Sound Designer Christopher Shutt

This adaptation is based on a literal translation from the Russian by Charlotte Pyke

Characters

Vassilly
father, a painting contractor

Akulina
mother, his wife

Tanya
their daughter, a teacher

Pyotr
their son, a law student, now expelled

Nil
their foster-son, a train driver

Polya
their servant, young

Stepanida
their servant, old

Perchikin
father of Polya, a birdcatcher

Teterev
lodger, a chorister

Elena
lodger, a widow

Shyshkin
friend of Pyotr's, a student

Tsvetaeva
friend of Tanya's, a teacher

Doctor

Old Crone, Old Man, Passers-by, Curious Folk, etc.

PHILISTINES

A forward slash (/) indicates that the next character's speech overlaps at this point. Where more than a single interruption occurs within the same speech, the points of overlap are indicated by (A), (B), (C), etc.

Act One

*The action takes place in the main living area of the
house of Vassilly Bessemenov. One gets the feeling he does
a lot of DIY, and Akulina, his wife, has certainly enjoyed
decorating the house over the years. It is a big house,
which sprawls and jumbles from room to room and floor
to floor. It is not, however, bohemian or messy in any
way. It is the house of people striving for betterment,
whilst being practical and sensible about their biggest
asset.*

*Twilight. Tanya is reading by the fading light, Polya is
sewing beside her.*

Tanya 'Strange, a moon, so small and sad and far away,
could shed light enough to smooth the broken ground
and still this restless river . . .'

She throws the book aside, disgusted.

It's too dark.

Polya stands obediently and makes for the lights.

Don't bother.

Polya I can turn on the lights.

Tanya I'm sick of it.

Polya Oh.

Quiet.

I was quite –
    It's well written, don't you think? Simple and sad. I was
hoping we'd – How does it end? Do they get married?

Tanya Is that the most a person can hope for?

Polya I wouldn't have married him. Too . . .

Quiet.

Tanya What?

Polya Boring. Complaining all the time, but not doing anything about it. You want a man who knows what he wants and knows how to get it. A confident man.

Tanya Is Nil one of those men?

Polya He's confident. Yes.

Tanya And, what does he want?

Polya He won't put up with – He won't let people get away with things. You see? Bad people. The wicked and the greedy won't do well by him. He doesn't like them. So.

Tanya Who is bad? Who is good? Who isn't wicked and greedy?

Polya Ah well. You see?

Quiet.

It's her that you want to know about, though. She's well written and interesting. Sweet. Attractive. You want to know about her and what will happen to her. It's a good story like that. For her. Because she's . . .

Tanya Polya, really.

She laughs at her.

You're so . . . There was no. Estate, no river, no moon. No. Such. Girl. At all. It's all made up. And irritating to add insult. Stupid and irritating. What life is like that? Writers never describe life as it is. Our life?

Polya They write about interesting things. / Not –

Tanya Books? Like this. These books are written by people who do not love me. Don't even like me. It's as if they are picking at me. 'This is better than you know. You? Oh, you don't know life at all.'

Polya I think you'd have to be amazing to be a writer. Thinking of all those different things.

Imagine meeting / a writer?

Tanya But they're wrong. Life is not at all. Special or tragic. I can tell you that, now. With the grand tone. No one declares their love to people – and it wouldn't *feel* the way they describe it, because they don't know, because it doesn't happen: because, it is all made up.

Life is not some tragic river. It's a big, murky ooze. Sludging monotonously onwards. Look too closely at the surface, and your head aches trying to detect any movement or anything interesting and worthwhile to actually say about it. That's life. Your head aching and throbbing with boredom and you don't even want to know why. No one wants to know, 'Why is the river flowing?'

Polya I wonder, what's he like? His hair? His clothes?

Tanya Who?

Polya The writer.

Tanya He's dead.

Polya Dead? Was he young?

Tanya Middle-aged. Vodka.

Polya Oh.

What is it about clever people and drink? That lodger of yours. He's clever. But he drinks. Why?

Tanya Why? Why? *Why?*

Life. Life, Polya. Is boring.

Pyotr appears in the gloom, rubbing his eyes.

Pyotr What time is it? Hello? Who's there?

Polya Me. And Tanya.

Pyotr What's with the dark?

Tanya We are lost in thought.

Pyotr I dreamt I was swimming. Water was like treacle. Difficult swimming, heavy. Looked up and couldn't work out which direction I was heading, couldn't see the banks. It was wide. A wide river. And . . . debris. There was stuff, coming towards me. Furniture. Mum and Dad's bed. Stuff. I reached out and it all fell away in my hands. Crumbled in my hands like teeth. Putrid and rotten.

I mean, really, you can't even get a break from this place by shutting your eyes.

What time is it? Any tea?

Polya stands.

Polya I'll see what Stepanida is doing.

She exits.

Pyotr This room is worse at night. If that's possible. It's somehow even more crowded, packed full of this old stuff. They seem to get bigger and heavier in the dark. Things. Can hardly breathe for things. Life moves on they say: go, tell it to the cupboard. Hasn't moved an inch in eighteen years. Still there, right where I bumped my head on it. Stubbed my toe. Get a move on. Do something, cupboard, do something else. Stupid, useless. It's not a cupboard, it's muttering . . . trying to tell me something.

What? Too busy being symbolic. Well, keep it to yourself. Shut your squeaking drawers.

Tanya Pyotr.
It's ridiculous. How boring this place makes you.

Pyotr As opposed / to you?

Tanya You don't do anything. You don't go anywhere. Upstairs to Lena's every night. Mum and Dad are . . .

Pyotr is pacing and whistling.

Anyway, I'm very tired all the time. I can't seem to . . .
    At school it's noise and confusion, so then I just long for peace and quiet, but I get here and there's this nothing. The nothing here, just –
    My thoughts go round and round. It's better since Lena moved in. She's cheerful. She's a cheerful soul. I'm very tired all the time, that's why . . . Pyotr. And the holidays are so far off – November. December. Even so –

The clock strikes six.

(*Over the clock.*) What would I hope for from holidays? Here? Pyotr?
    I'm glad you're back.

Vassilly sticks his head in.

Vassilly Surprise, surprise. Talk, talk. talk. Have you found the time in all your talk to collect / that rent for me?

Pyotr I'll do it. I'm doing it.

Vassilly Make sure you do.

He is gone again.

Tanya What are you doing?

Pyotr Just. Dad wanted me to make sure everyone's, you know.

Tanya You're studying to be a lawyer, not a –

Pyotr I'm suspended and. While I'm here. He asked. What?

Akulina bustles in. She begins setting the table.

7

Akulina It's raining again.

Tanya Did you go to Lena's last night?

Pyotr nods and picks at something. Akulina is watching as she sets the table.

Was it fun?

Pyotr It's cold in here.

Akulina It's cold in here. We had the heating on earlier. But it's still cold.

Tanya What did you do?

Pyotr You know, drank tea, sang. Argued.

Akulina It's an / old house. Draughty.

Tanya Who did you end up arguing with?

Pyotr Nil and Shyshkin.

Akulina Father's angry again. His back / hurts.

Tanya So predictable.

Pyotr Yes, but with Nil. Nil particularly. His ecstasies about life. Always preaching optimism and the future, it's a joke.

Akulina Backs are tricky things, as / you get older.

Pyotr Hearing him, you'd think life was like some long-lost American uncle who will shower you with unexpected wealth.

Akulina He's old, of course. You can't have a young back for ever. And then there's / the usual bad debts and disorder.

Tanya And Shyshkin? What was his problem?

Akulina Our expenses are enormous. It's / a worry.

Pyotr Shyshkin? The benefits of milk and the dangers of tobacco. Or something.

Yes, and he said I was developing a bourgeois way of thinking.

Tanya Nothing new, then?

Do you really like Lena? . . . She's. I mean? Lena?

Pyotr She's not bad. She's cheerful. She's all right. She's fun.

Akulina Fun? Fun? Fun all right – she's a spinning top. No purpose in life. Every day God gives her she's about having guests and endless parties and sweets and dancing and songs. All that carrying on upstairs. Why can't she find the time to buy herself a washbasin, then? She uses a bowl to wash in. A bowl. So the water is all over the floorboards. It's rotting the floor. She'll rot right through the floor with all her dirty ways.

Silence. Tanya continues her conversation with her brother.

Tanya I was at school last night. Helping with the appeal. Somov, he's one of the trustees, didn't even say hello to me. I've been there fourteen hours straight by this stage; teaching all day and then doing the event.

So Sonya Kardov, whose main achievement as far as I can tell is that she is Judge Romanov's mistress, well, she saunters in and Somov's all over her. Anyone would've thought the Tsarina herself had walked in. A trumped / up tart.

Akulina People just don't know anything about manners / and respect.

Tanya You just would expect. No one cares about teachers, but some tart all painted up like a doll? Just because she might have access to a bit of money.

9

Pyotr You have to rise above that stuff. He's got no class, no matter how many boards he sits on. You can't be surprised, though, the point of / the evening was to raise money.

Akulina His sister is insulted and he doesn't even rush to her defence. It shouldn't / matter what the money –

Pyotr Mum, really. Keep out of it.

Tanya You can't have a conversation when she's around. Not allowed to pursue a line of thought in this house. God forbid.

Akulina Now, now. Let's not get snappy. Everybody. Smiles.

Stepanida drags in the samovar.

Pyotr, help Stepanida with the samovar, there's a / good lad.

Stepanida Somebody, please. I haven't the strength in my bones for this contraption any more.

Akulina We're not employing another servant just to carry the samovar.

Stepanida Get one of your lodgers to help, then. Pyotr, give us a hand getting this thing on the table, it'll break my arms.

Pyotr helps lift the samovar. It's heavy. Stepanida goes.

Akulina Petya? See if you can get Teterev to help / with the samovar.

Tanya Mum, really. Not this again.

Pyotr Will I ask him to fetch the water and cut the wood while I'm at it?

Tanya Petya.

Akulina I don't know why you're both so touchy, the samovar / is heavy. He's a big –

Pyotr The bloody samovar. Every evening you go on and on about the bloody / samovar. The solution is simple – get another servant.

Akulina Don't swear.
  We don't need another servant. Your father does the wood and the water. I do the linen.

Pyotr You're a miser. You are misers. Both of you are misers. / You've got money –

Akulina Shh. Your father will hear. Then you'll get 'miser' all right.
  'Miser'?

Pyotr Well, you have the / money.

Tanya Pyotr. Drop it. Please. I can't bear it. She does this.

Pyotr Yes, she just . . . before I realise, she just –

Akulina Who's she? The cat's mother?

Pyotr Day in. Day out. This stupid quarrelling. It's like lead. I can't / move. I can't think.

Akulina (*calling over*) Dad, time for tea, pet!

Pyotr When my university suspension is up I'm straight back to Moscow. And I'm going to work hard. Maybe I'll come home for a week every now and then. But no more. I tell you, Tanya, after three years of living on my own I can't do this rubbish here any more. Trivial, bourgeois rubbish. I tell you, get away, away from the boring –

Tanya Where? Where can I go?

Pyotr Study.

Tanya I don't want to study. I want to live. I want to live, Pyotr.

Akulina is arranging the tea things. In doing so, she burns the soft skin on the inside of her arm on the samovar. She lets out an exclamation of pain. Tanya and Pyotr continue oblivious.

Pyotr? I don't know . . . I can't imagine what it means to live. What do I do? To live?

Pyotr Well you have to . . . live. Skilfully. Carefully. You have to.
Live . . . ? You just –

Akulina Petya, sweet? Fetch your da.

Pyotr Yes, Mum.

Pyotr goes. Vassilly comes in at another door.

Vassilly This is lump sugar. I've / told you –

Tanya Come on, Daddy.

Vassilly Keep out of it. Makes no difference to you, you don't pay for it. You just see it all there, laid out waiting for you. It's not free. / Nothing's free.

Akulina I bought a little. Now let's not get angry. I bought a little to tide / us over.

Vassilly I'm not angry. Lump sugar is a waste of money, that's all. It's heavier than normal sugar and it isn't as sweet. So you pay more to use more. Yeah? You don't need an education to work that one out.
Look at the face on it. What are you frowning about?

Tanya Nothing.

Vassilly Nothing? No wonder she's not married, if she pulls faces over nothing.

Akulina Dad. Come on, please.

Vassilly Scowls whenever I come into the room. I'm only trying to help her. Teach them the ins and outs. You think I carp on about this stuff for my own sake? I'm trying to teach you how to live. And I have to say, I look at you and your brother and I can't imagine how you think you are going to live. What are you aiming for? Clearly you don't like the way we do things – OK, OK, we can see that. We aren't as stupid as you think. We may not have finished our school and paid enormous amounts of money – Enormous Amounts of Money – to learn this and that theory on whatever, but we at least had a plan for our lives. A set of values. A way of living. I just wonder, I worry, what exactly do you expect to do? / What's your plan?

Tanya I've heard all this before.

Vassilly So have I, Tanya. So have I. 'Cause I've been saying it for years. And I won't stop saying it till I die, because I'm worried. I worry sick about you. Mum and I broke our backs to get you educated and set up properly, and what have we? A son who is expelled from university for disruptive – subversions. And, and a daughter who is a scowling old maid?

Akulina Father.

Vassilly What? A spade's a spade.

Tanya I work . . . I . . .

Vassilly But who cares, Tanya? (*A*) Twenty-five roubles a month? No one (*B*) needs your measly twenty-five roubles. For God's sake get married and I'll (*C*) pay you fifty to shut up about it.

Akulina (*overlapping at A*) Father? (*Overlapping at B.*) Dear? (*Overlapping at C.*) Father?

Look. Look. I made curd tarts.

Vassilly Curd tarts.

She'll do anything to protect you children from the truth. She's worried I'll scare you away. Bring them out. Lets have curd tarts then, Mum.

He takes the lid off the tin. Perchikin appears in the doorway.

Oh no. It's the bird man. There's the lid.

Perchikin makes an elaborate bow as Akulina hides away the tarts.

Perchikin Bless this house, it's silver-haired master and his gorgeous lady-wife. Bless their gentle, honourable offspring for all time immemorial.

Vassilly Someone's been drinking.

Perchikin For sorrow, dear / friend.

Vassilly What sorrow?

Perchikin No one knows the sorrow of the bird man.

Vassilly God help us.

Perchikin I sold a chaffinch today. Cutest little darling, yodelled like a goatherd. Three years together, and I sell her for a couple of pieces of silver. I feel bad for doing it. Bad for the little warbler. I loved that bird.

Vassilly Why'd you sell it?

Perchikin Got an offer I couldn't refuse.

Akulina What do you need money for? You only spend it on drink.

Perchikin True. True enough. In one hand, out the other.

Vassilly All the more reason to keep hold of your precious bird.

Perchikin It's not that simple.
She was going blind. She was on her last legs.

Vassilly laughs a hard, bitter laugh.

See? I sell what I love? And people laugh.

Pyotr and Teterev enter.

Tanya Is Nil back?

Pyotr He's at a rehearsal with Shyshkin.

Vassilly Where are they doing this play?

Pyotr It's for the soldiers.

Perchikin Noble, noble. The noble arts. Do you want to catch a tit or two, Teterev? This is the weather for it.

Teterev When?

Perchikin Why wait? Tomorrow?

Teterev I can't tomorrow. Funeral at eleven.

Perchikin We could try for dawn? Early, any rate.

Teterev If I'm up, drop by. Akulina Ivanovna? Is there anything left over from lunch?

Akulina A little. Polya, dear?

Polya heads off obediently.

Teterev Sung at a funeral and a wedding today. The full gamut of the human experience from the ridiculous to the utterly pointless.

A silence settles on the room. Pyotr drifts away with his tea.

Vassilly Been a good few weeks for you.

Teterev Yes, they're busy this month, humans. If they're not getting married they're dying.

Vassilly Good month for saving.

Akulina Do all those lovely weddings get you thinking about your own future? / Terenty?

Tanya Mum.

Teterev The future? It's all funerals.

Tanya slopes off to talk with Pyotr.

Perchikin Don't get married. No reason to bother. Better off catching bullfinches. The bullfinch is the king of birds.

Teterev Hear, hear.

Polya comes in with the food.

Perchikin Fat little buggers, popping with life. You get those mornings. Snow thick on the ground. Pure silence. Your heart aches with the joy, crystal clear blue sky, trees just breaking into leaf. The branches still dusted with a light blessing of snow. When in a whirl a flock of the little bastards appears, zipping between the branches, frolicking in the light snow. It's like fragments of your soul at play. I'd turn into a bullfinch, dive into the snow with them . . .

Vassilly The bullfinch is the stupidest bird.

Perchikin I think so, I think so.

Teterev Lucky bullfinch.

Perchikin I love catching birds. What song in the world is better than birdsong?

Polya You're still a boy, Dad.

Vassilly It's probably a sin to net those innocent birds. Have you thought of that?

Perchikin Every day, every day, Vassilly. But what else can I do? I'm a man with no talents to talk of and no skills to make up for it. I love it and surely anything done with love is blessed?

Vassilly Anything?

Perchikin Anything.

Vassilly What if I love to nick other people's property?

Perchikin Well that's. That's stealing. Breaking the Ten Commandments is different.

Pyotr I'm sure the birds might have something to say about it. As God's creatures.

Perchikin That's harsh.

Akulina lets out a big yawn.

Akulina Ooh. This is all a bit high and mighty for me. Play some guitar, Terenty.

Tanya Mum.

Akulina What?
   What? All I can do is sit with my mouth buttoned up, then.

Vassilly Oh yes, Mum, careful, we're among the learned ones now. They can criticise and theorise all they like – talk, talk, talk – with their scientific powers but you and I? / No, we're supposed to shut up and shoulder the burden.

Tanya Petya didn't say . . .

Vassilly Too old and / stupid we are.

Akulina Come on, Dad, we're all just having a chat. / No one said that. She didn't say –

Perchikin We are old, my friend. That's what makes us stupid.

Akulina / No one said old and stupid.

Vassilly Speak for yourself.

Perchikin No, no. Seriously. I would go so far as to say if there were no old people there would be no stupidity in the world. When we think, it is like trying to light a fire with green wood. All smoke and no heat.

Teterev He's on to something.

Vassilly What's this / load of –

Perchikin It's the stubbornness does it to us. An old man can see he's making a mistake, he knows by this time in his life he doesn't understand anything, but he's just too stubborn to admit it. He's lived, he says. 'I've lived,' when all he's really done is wear out forty pair of trousers – but oh no, he can't let that be all. No, no. 'I'm old,' he says. 'I know. I'm right.' But understanding, you see? No, the old mind is too heavy and addled with complications to understand. The young mind is quick and light.

Akulina Anyway –

Vassilly That all just sounds like – bloody smoke. You have to get to the bottom of that. If old people are stupid? Then surely they would be the ones sent to school.

Akulina There you are.

Perchikin No point. No point / training old dogs.

Vassilly Don't interrupt me. I was making a point myself. My point. I'm older than you? And that counts for something. Doesn't it? See? And if it didn't, then I wouldn't be able to say it. Would I?

Akulina That's right.

Vassilly If these young minds are so busy being light and brilliant, why don't they want to talk to us? And learn some of our experience? If they are so smart, hey? Think about that.

Akulina I don't think / he meant . . .

Vassilly And I will. Shut up, woman. I'll think about it. I suppose you all think it doesn't matter what I think about? I'm too old and stupid to know anything and have these sorts of conversations . . .

He stands and makes to leave the room.

Too stupid for my own learned bloody children.

He goes.

Perchikin You shouldn't insult your father.

Pyotr It was you.

Perchikin Me? I've never insulted a soul.

Akulina Did we need to talk about being old? And you two could've . . . I don't know why we try and talk about all this nonsense? It's not for us, talk is for aristocrats on estates . . . He's an old man with a sore back who has worked hard. You should respect him . . . just for that . . .
And then, anyway, he is your father.

Tanya What's he so angry about?

Akulina Well, perhaps you should spend even more time away from him. Will that help, do you think? To find out?

She follows after Vassilly.
Polya begins clearing the table under Teterev's watchful eye. Tanya drifts off.

Polya What are you staring at?

Teterev You.

Perchikin Petya, I've been meaning to ask for a long time. What is a sewage system?

Pyotr Why?
It would take too long to explain and I don't know that you'd understand.

Perchikin Try me.

Pyotr It's too boring.

Perchikin Do you know? Does he know?

Polya Where's Nil?

Teterev You have delicate hands.

Polya Yesterday it was eyes.

Teterev Who knows what tomorrow holds?

Polya Why?

Teterev Perhaps you think I'm in love with you?

Polya God. I leave thinking to you people.

Teterev Well, at least have a think about that.

Polya What?

Teterev Why am I here?

Polya To be weird.

Teterev I know. You've told me that.
Leave. Leave this house, it's bad for you. There's nothing here.

Pyotr Is this a love scene? Should I make an exit?

Teterev No, I don't consider you part of the cast.

Pyotr What's that supposed to mean?

Polya You're a bully.

Teterev That's new.

Teterev drifts away. Tanya returns, standing in a doorway.

Tanya Where's Nil, then?

She drifts back into the room and over to the piano.

Perchikin Apparently, in England, they've built ships that fly. Just recently. I read it somewhere. You sit in it, push a button and bang – you are right there, up above the birds. Above the clouds, above . . . up?

Scores of the English have disappeared.

Is that possible, Petya?

Pyotr It's rubbish.

Perchikin It was in print.

Pyotr They'll print anything.

Perchikin Wouldn't they draw the line at that?

Pyotr What?

Perchikin That.

Tanya has begun to play something sad on the piano.

I think everyone is sick of me. We should go, Pelegaya.

Polya I'll just clear up.

Perchikin Do you remember catching bullfinches with me, Petya? You loved me then.

Pyotr I do still.

Perchikin Do you think so? No.

Pyotr I do still. It's different.

I loved lollies and gingerbread then. But now . . . I don't ever eat them. That's all . . .

Perchikin I understand. Time passes.

Terenty? Beer?

Teterev Not for me

Perchikin Well. It's cheerful in the bar, any rate. People in this house need to do something. Even just a hobby. By Jesus, a game of cards'd be a start.

Anyone? No takers?
You sure about that drink?

Teterev Have a good one.

*Perchikin exits. Tanya continues the piece she is
playing. Offstage something crashes to the floor and
Stepanida and Akulina have words.*

Tanya Where's Nil? Why so long to get here?

Pyotr What time is it?

Tanya Elena?

Pyotr Sorry?

Silence. Just the piano.

Teterev No one will come here.

Tanya You're always so gloomy.

Teterev No one will come here because there is nothing
here.

Pyotr So says the Great Sage Terenty.

Teterev Perchikin is alive. But you, both standing on the
threshold of life, you are already half dead.

Pyotr What does that make you?

Tanya Can we stop this, please?

Pyotr Amazing. This / role you play. This role of judge.

Tanya Enough.

Pyotr But why us, in particular? Are we any worse than
any other family?

Teterev That's hardly the point.

Tanya Stop it.

Pyotr What? You love us so much you want to save us?

Teterev Oh, no. I don't like you at all.

Quiet.

Pyotr Well, at least we've cleared that up.

Polya comes in.

Polya I want to go and see a show. Anyone?

Teterev What is it?

Polya *The Joys of Our Youth*. Tanya?

Teterev What? Shouting, wailing, sobbing. People leaping on and off horses, brandishing guns and other great truths? Not Tanya.

Teterev is at the piano, sporadically drumming out big sombre notes.

Tanya Life breaks people noiselessly, without shouting, without tears, without horses . . . unnoticed.

Polya Pyotr?

Pyotr Youth?

Polya *The Joys of Our Youth.*

Pyotr Is it set in the heart of someone standing between 'I want' and 'I should', being gradually torn to pieces? That's youth.

Teterev Bit short on the 'joy' there, Petya.

Polya It's not meant to be serious. It's theatre. Everything doesn't have to be serious. Think of Don Sezan de Bazan, the true Spanish nobleman. You can have a hero.

Teterev I'm like him, people say.

Polya You?

Teterev No?

Tanya When they say they love each other on stage you're supposed to believe it. That's how it works. But why should you? When it doesn't happen. It. Does. Not. Happen, Polya. So why? *Why* should I sit there in the dark, pretending it does?

Polya Don't then, fine . . . I'm going anyway. Terenty?

Teterev Only if you say I'm like Don Cesar de . . . whoever he was.

Polya You aren't.

Polya exits.

Pyotr What does she get from a dumpy old poof pretending to be heroic?

Teterev Possibility?

Tanya A long cape, lined in red silk.

Teterev Lightness of heart. Villains are never cheery.

Tanya Which makes you evil incarnate.

Teterev I'm not ambitious enough to be evil. I'm a drunk and no more.

Quiet.

That's popular these days. We have no time any more for anyone with anything of value to offer. Innovators. Leaders. Heroes. It's all hail the villains and the slackers. The petty thief and the backsliding murderer. That's the craze these days. Hope is seen as an attempt to sell somebody something. That's what makes it so hard to be young. The young these days are so old.

Pyotr 'The young'? Who are we? What are we? To / say anything about these days so definitely.

Teterev (*singing to his piano*) 'We are all wild as the wind. We are as freeee as birds.'

Tanya Stop that horrible dirge.

Teterev Don't shoot me.

Tanya stands and leaves.

Pyotr But what in God's name is 'young'? What does that word conjure up? It's empty, and I don't know what it would take to fill it. Actually fill it with some kind of genuine representative. Meaning? Authority? Purpose.
So it –

Silence. Teterev continues on the piano.

There are so many words that just get spoken and you don't even think about what they are trying to say. What's hidden inside them and beneath them. What I think they mean and then, what someone else thinks. Jesus . . . I mean . . .
'Life'? As fundamental a word as that.
My . . . life. What's in there? What's that mean?

Teterev fills the room with the sound of groaning strings.

What was I thinking? I went to university to study. Why didn't I just study? Why did I get all caught up in demonstrations and . . .
Can you stop that? Please?
You know, I didn't really feel like there was some 'regime' at work preventing me from studying Roman Law. Honestly. I didn't feel the censorship and the oppression. I felt . . . The regime I felt actually – and gave in to – was the regime of my peers. And now two years of my life have been wasted. Sure. That's force. That's an oppressive regime. Against me. But I didn't feel it before I went kicking at it. Why didn't I just study like a student instead

25

of getting all caught up in . . . getting all lost in the feelings of other people? Other people's ideas.

My idea was simple, you know. Go to university, study, become a lawyer, read, observe. Just live. My life. Not some other.

Teterev Sounds exactly like your parents' lives. Even though you can't stand them. Sounds to me like the only ones who'll benefit from your life are the Church and the State. They couldn't care less. Didn't you know? Your great idea of life? The silent humble servant of a rapidly disintegrating society? That's it? That's all you've come up with?

Pyotr Society. There's no such thing as society. It's only what people try and convince you it means. 'A person must be a citizen first and foremost.' My comrades screamed at each other, screamed into each other's faces. That was society. That was society right there. I felt it. Then suddenly, behind me: 'A person must obey the law.' Others were shouting over us. What law? What law? The law students' law or the others' law? All I learnt from my radical student experience? Society is just an obstacle to me. I am an individual. A free individual.

Listen.

Would you stop that horrible noise and listen?

Teterev I've been accompanying you, doing the accidental radicalisation of the former-citizen, uptight-bourgeois, moaning ex-student foxtrot . . . for what? Half an hour?

Pyotr I was talking. Trying to . . .

Silence. Teterev returns his attention to the piano.
Suddenly Nil, Elena, Shyshkin and Tsvetaeva pour in, all full of light and youth and joie de vivre. Followed by Tanya.

Elena Who's died?

Teterev Pyotr. Who was almost interesting.

Elena Hello, sweet man. It's all right, you know, to be 'almost' when you're young.
Has the lodger been awful?

Teterev Me?

Nil Terenty?

Teterev crosses to Nil and they discuss something quickly in a whisper. Teterev agrees to whatever it is.

Tsvetaeva The rehearsal was fabulous. Darlings.

Elena And what about that Lieutenant Bykov?

Shyshkin Bovine Bykov. He of the / cow's eyes.

Elena Little Almost? My sweet? He was making the most ferocious advances towards me.

Pyotr What do you want me to do about it?

Elena Oops, someone's in a stink.

Tsvetaeva Again?

Shyshkin Our Almost is almost ever thus.

Elena And Tanya?

Tanya Call me Always. Ever. / Thus.

Elena Come on, everybody. I manage to be cheerful. Why am I able to be cheerful?

Nil I am too. I think it's 'cause we don't try and think about it.

Tsvetaeva Well, here's to not thinking about it.

Shyshkin It depends, but tonight – we dance.

Elena But I did think about it – and I still feel happy. Always do. How can that be, wise lodger?

Teterev You are frivolity incarnate.

Shyshkin / Possibly so.

Elena I'll remind you of that when you finally declare your love to me.

Nil I need to eat. I'm due back at work soon.

Tsvetaeva Another shift?

Nil I did twenty-four hours straight a couple of days ago. I'll see what Stepanida's up to.

Tanya I'll fetch her. For you.

Tanya and Nil exit.

Teterev Haven't I already declared my love to you?

Elena In between prophecies of doom. Maybe?

Teterev I'll have another bash at it. There was a time in my life when I was in love with two girls and a married woman all at the same time.

Elena And . . . ?

Teterev Too much hard work.

Elena What did you do to upset Pyotr?

Teterev moves away with a laugh and Elena follows. They talk quietly, glancing at Pyotr from time to time. Shyshkin meanwhile sidles up to Pyotr.

Shyshkin How are you?

Pyotr Yeah, you know.

Shyshkin My boots have come apart. Again. Could you lend me a couple of roubles? Just for three days?

Pyotr That'll be seven you owe me.

Shyshkin Three days, I get paid.

Tsvetaeva Pyotr, why don't you help us with the plays?

Pyotr I don't act.

Shyshkin Hey? Neither do we.

Tsvetaeva You could try it. The soldiers are not bad people. They are . . . Everyone's doing their best. Shirkov is funny. There's a gentleness under / all that. Bravado.

Shyshkin Shirkov's not the only one. They don't really understand how the regime is using them.

Pyotr Don't they? Poor things. Tell me? How is that interesting, though? Not understanding? Isn't that good old ignorance?

Tsvetaeva What are you all of a sudden? These people need to / be made aware. That's why.

Teterev has erupted from behind them, staring at Pyotr.

Teterev Pity? No, no, no.

Elena Shh, let's just . . .

Elena winds him back into a quiet discussion.

Pyotr I'm bourgeois. Apparently. Just a bourgeois.

Shyshkin You can't just pretend you don't know what's going on.

Pyotr Pretend? Who says you know . . .

Again the discussion erupts from behind them.

Teterev I don't want pity so / why would I –

Elena I'm just saying. Anyway, shouldn't we pay evil with good? Isn't that best? Turn the other cheek.

Teterev Cheek, really? Sorry.

Elena Shhh. All right. All right.

Elena moves away from him and rejoins the group.

Pyotr Actually . . . pretend . . .? Why do you pretend to sympathise with these people? These Good Soldiers who would be your enemy / in reality.

Elena We're not pretending. Getting to know people?

Pyotr / Flirting.

Shyshkin We are all connected. Under the uniform. And as you get to know them / you realise they are actually very straightforward.

Tsvetaeva If you bothered. That's very arrogant.

Pyotr Didn't I tell you? I am an arrogant bourgeois. Ask my indentured friend here.

Shyshkin It'd do you good. They are healthy. Truer than you and I. And we aren't so different from each / other, by the way.

Pyotr You are living a lie. You go to your good honest soldiers. Patronising them with your secret aim of bringing them round to your ideas. Ridiculous, overblown rubbish ambitions. Reinventing your soldiers with good will and theatre?

Tsvetaeva We're doing something. This / is something.

Pyotr Something? Fooling yourselves. If. If you could get through to those pig-ignorant morons. Even if. The next day their commanding officer would beat it out of them. Beat out of their empty heads the tiny ideas you spent all that time trying to stuff in there. And this is if. *If* your ideas are of any value in the first place.

Tsvetaeva You and your – This is just another one . . . You.

Shyshkin Pyotr. This is somewhere that you are . . . You are letting yourself . . . We need to sit down and have a good talk. Where is / all this bitterness coming from?

Pyotr We talked last night.
Bitter?

Shyshkin It won't do you any good. Thinking like this.

Pyotr Any good?

Elena Why are you pretending? Do you want us to think you are some dreadful conservative . . .

Pyotr I'm just marking out my territory. / What I have come to believe. From experience.

Tsvetaeva He thinks he's being clever. All men try to be what they think is clever or interesting. This one acts the pessimist. This one . . . acts his father.

Pyotr What's / that –

Teterev Guilty on both counts.

Tsvetaeva You sound like your old man. Sorry.

Pyotr How does that . . . ?

Teterev is laughing. Tsvetaeva is on him.

Tsvetaeva And you.

Teterev Me? Oh no, you've got me all worked out. I accept.
As the local pessimist, can I wonder?

Tsvetaeva Make a joke of it.

Teterev Someone once asked me to pay evil with good. And I'm puzzled. What's the exchange rate?

Elena Don't be mean. He's / just trying to –

Shyshkin Wait, don't stop him. I love it when he talks.
Our ideas . . . We all deal in old currency. Lets see if he
can mint something new from good and evil.

Pyotr At least you realise the ideas you peddle are second
hand.

Shyshkin I never claimed to have had an original thought.
But I'd like to.

Teterev Congratulations.

Shyshkin What?

Teterev You just did.

Shyshkin Well . . . But that was an accident.

Teterev You can't do it on purpose. I tried for years.

Elena Get on with it. Why can't we repay evil with
good?

> *Shyshkin begins making a noise of trumpets as if to
> herald something great. Or perhaps he imitates a drum
> roll – something sort of young and festive.*

Teterev Earthlings. Bipeds all. The opposite of Good is . . .

> *Several of the gathered listeners respond as if in class.*

Several Evil. Yes.

Teterev Bravo. The great mistake you all make is to
assume that because something is opposite, it is in some
way equivalent. If a right-handed man were to choose
which hand he would lose, my guess is he would choose –
his left. In order to make this new-style economics of
morality work, we must find the essential value of each
quality. Agreed?
    And are we all agreed that availability is one of the
driving forces in any economy?

They are.

Evil, then? Is everywhere. Common as mud, it abounds in nature and thrives in people. Evil is, like dirt, essentially worthless.

Good, however, is a man-made quality, rare and precious. Possibly even priceless. There is nothing better on Earth. It is therefore impossible to balance evil and good in some kind of metaphysical market place. Good can only be used to pay for good. And the payments must be exact, or man's natural greed will cause him to seek more when he can and complain when he does not. Pay for good with good, but only as much good as you received. No more and of course no less.

The only currency you can use when trading in evil is evil because nothing else is as low and worthless. And evil is in constant inflation. Remember: always pay a hundred times over for evil. Reward the man who does you evil with as much evil as you can muster and be rid of it. If he gave you stone when you begged for bread? Bring the whole crushing mountain down on his stupid, pig-ignorant head.

Silence. The darkness in Teterev has swamped the gathering.

Elena You've suffered a lot at the hands of other people.

Teterev But how happy it makes me knowing they will suffer so much more from me. In time.

Nil comes in with a bowl of soup and wedge of bread. Tanya follows behind him.

Nil You've confused thinking with understanding. Always making philosophies from daily trivialities. When it's raining? It's raining and nothing else. I can't help it, sorry – you are an example of over-education being mistaken for good education.

33

Tanya Nil. That's so . . . / rude.

Nil What? If you find life boring? Do something, there's nothing else can be said. If it's tough at home, go away.

Elena Let him have it. You'd be doing us all a favour to knock this one down a peg or two.

Nil This one? Fancies himself a great satirist.

Teterev Call me Swift, please.

Nil Swift? No, oh no – he managed to achieve something. He put pen to paper.

Pyotr / Exactly.

Teterev A hit. A palpable hit.
    And . . .?

Nil Nice soup.

He looks around at everybody: they are all staring at him, wanting something from him.

So . . .? Was Polya here? I mean . . . Where's she gone?

Tanya To the theatre.
    Do you need her?

Nil No. I don't . . . Not right now. But you know –

Everyone smiles except Tanya.

Tanya No?

Nil returns to his food.

No. I don't know.

Elena What happened in the kitchen? To make Nil so rude?

Tsvetaeva What did you quarrel over, Tanya?

Shyshkin My favourite thing about Nil is his musical genius.

Pyotr No, no, the way he eats. Just / so –

Nil Everything I do. I try and do well.

Elena Tanya?

Tanya Nothing. I don't want to.

Tsvetaeva You never want to do anything.

Tanya How do you know? Maybe I really want to die.

Tsvetaeva / Tanya, yuk.

Elena Not death tonight.

Nil Death, death, death. Death is another pointless thing to carp on. There's nothing to be said about death until you die.

Teterev Or not.

Elena Right. Let's all go to mine. The samovar is calling.

Shyshkin And a bite to eat? Dare one hope?

Elena I'll rustle something up.

Shyshkin Watching him eat has made me ravenous.

Nil I could eat it all again. Let's go.

Tanya Aren't you due back at work?

Nil I've an hour.

Tanya Shouldn't you rest?

Nil Rest?

Elena Pyotr? Will you join us?

Pyotr . . . Almost, dancing.

Elena Definitely footloose.

Tsvetaeva Take your partners. Nil, you're mine.

*Nil joins Tsvetaeva. The others have formed up.
Shyshkin takes Tanya's hand. Teterev is alone.*

Shyshkin You're with me, then.

Teterev As usual. They say there are more women on
Earth than men, yet every town I've been in, there was
never a woman left over for me.

*Elena starts marching in an exaggerated Christopher
Robin march and belts out the Marseillaise joyfully.*

Elena '*Allons enfants de la Patrie . . .*'

Shyshkin whacks Pyotr on the back affectionately.

Shyshkin Get a wriggle on then, my favourite Son of the
Fatherland.

*They exit noisily, singing and laughing.
Tanya is alone. The party is now banging on
overhead.
Blackout.*

Act Two

The same. Autumn. Midday. Vassilly is at the table,
Tanya pacing silently, Pyotr staring out of a window.

Vassilly I've been talking for an hour and we . . . I don't.
I don't understand. Can you at least look at me? Tanya,
sit down. Please.

Tanya sits. Pyotr turns in to the room.

Pyotr What do you want?

Vassilly I want to understand. What your aims are? Who
you are? My own dear children / who –

Pyotr Well, give us a chance. You'll see if you let us be. If
you let me finish studying, / you'll see.

Vassilly Studying? Exactly. You were, but now what are
you doing? / Messing around.

Pyotr I have to get back in. The suspension . . .

Vassilly Back to more study? But for what? All it seems
to have done is made you resent the world. Resent what
your mother and I have strived so hard for. All this learning
has just made you hate us. Why do you hate us? You think
it was unfair they threw you out of university? / I would
have, too – going on about what's best for the world.
How would you know?

Pyotr Well, it was . . .

Vassilly Tell me? How you would know? A student is
there to learn, not to teach. If every lad of twenty thought
he knew best, then everything would be arse-about.

Excuse me. If you know best, why don't you even know who you are? Study? By all means study if you are prepared to *learn*. Study away, because when you are disciplined, then perhaps you can become the master. But until then, Pyotr? You do as you are told. That's how it works.

Akulina is in.

Akulina Dad? Should we think / about dinner?

Vassilly Shut up. Don't stick your nose in here, we're talking.

Akulina leaves. Tanya stands again and begins pacing the room.

Education? Is a bollocks is all I can see.

Neither of you tell me. Neither of you say what you're thinking. Neither of you give me a hug any more. Neither of you say, 'Good morning Dad, how are you?' You scowl at me and skulk away like I'm a stranger in the house, ruining your fun. And that hurts. Look at Tanya, withering, a scowling old maid. That's an embarrassment amongst my friends, did you think of that? I don't say she was the greatest beauty in the world, but I can provide a dowry. I would have thought the man lucky to be welcomed into this family. I've seen girls as plain get well married and that's without the sort of dowry I have to offer. And I wanted you to be a lawyer, Pyotr: a member of the town council, an esteemed citizen. A man, Pyotr, proud of his father and a man I could be proud of. Filip Nazarov's son. *Finished* his study, got married, took a dowry, earns upwards of two thousand a year. Already. Filip Nazarov's son, more than two thousand a year. He'll be on the council by the time he's thirty, mark my words. Filip Nazarov, who's just . . . Filip Nazarov . . . I mean. He's a bore and second rate. His son. Well, he must be . . . That's a happy family. That's another hurt.

Tanya This is torture. *Torture.*

Vassilly What's it supposed to be? Some kind of hobby?

Tanya We want different / things from you.

Vassilly What do you want? Exactly. I don't know what you want. What do you want?

Tanya He just wants – He's going to study. If you leave him alone.

Vassilly If I leave him alone he'll be hooked up with that hussy. / I know what she's about.

Pyotr Don't call her that.
   You can't call someone that.

Vassilly She's a widow, son. Call a spade a spade. / And don't think she has any real fondness for you.

Pyotr That's just rubbish. That's just. This sort of . . . What are you talking about?

Tanya Don't / fall for it, Petya.

Vassilly She wants a rent-free house. She wants / to get away with it.

Pyotr / You've got a completely different. Reality. You live in . . .

Tanya Petya, don't.

Vassilly Reality? A different reality? There is only one reality, or haven't you got round to / that little fact yet?

Pyotr That's where you're wrong.

Vassilly Because you are studying? You choose reality now, do you? In the middle of your different realities, are we? Why don't you just close your eyes and see if I disappear. If this is all some . . . other reality. / Hopeless load of . . .

Tanya What he meant, Dad. He meant the things. The truths that you / hold on to. The truths that you hold on to. What you believe? Doesn't apply to us. It's not what we believe.

Vassilly What he meant was a load of rubbish.

Pyotr I don't know what you are so uptight about.

Vassilly Believe? You believe? What do you believe? You people don't believe in anything. That you can even say, that you can think, that what I believe differs from what you believe. Proves, exactly, that you have no *real* belief because everyone knows that there is only *one way to believe*. That's what belief is. You have no faith, no fear. *No morals*. You drift around and waste away your whole life and tell me now you have something you believe in? What do you believe in? What do you genuinely . . . I mean . . . This is the world. This is the time and the day and the . . . this is *it*. What else can you believe? What can you in this other reality possibly believe? This is it.

Akulina pokes her head in.

Akulina Dad, please, can we stop now?

Vassilly Stop? *Stop?* You can't just stop. These people are – Get out of here.

Akulina I'm just trying.

Pyotr Don't take it out on her. She's just –

Akulina / Pyotr.

Vassilly Are you running this household? This degree of yours is, is, is a degree in running lives and telling people what's reality?

Pyotr Father, you have to understand / this is unnecessary.

Tanya / Somebody STOP.

Vassilly I have to understand? Surely I'm / too stupid.

Pyotr Why are you doing this? Suddenly and / for no reason. No *real reason*.

Vassilly Suddenly? Suddenly? Are you / blind? This has been building in here. In here for ages.

Tanya This is rubbish.

Akulina (*simultaneously*) Petya, please. Give in, darling.

Vassilly Building and building.

Tanya Pyotr? Leave. Calm down, Father. / Calm down.

Akulina Tanya, have some respect.

Vassilly THIS IS MY HOUSE. This is my house. I am your father. You bloody well respect me and do as I say. Already I. I am the one. *It is me*, young man. Me, that is helping clear your name with the police, after your ridiculous demonstration – against what? It's me, backing you with my reputation. *Me*, who pays your fees at university so you can squander your time on these fanciful societies and – learning what? WHAT? I'll tell you what – *learn this*: this is my house and I will tell who is who and who is what and you can go be damned the lot of you.

The door bursts open and Nil, dirty from work, steams in.

Nil I need twenty kopeks for the cab. Quick. Anyone? Did I interrupt something?

Vassilly Take your hat off.

Akulina Bursts in here straight into the living room, all dirty from work.

Nil Don't take it out on me. / I work.

Pyotr Here. Hurry back.

Nil To take the heat off you? Great.

And he disappears again.

Vassilly Rushes in. Takes what he likes. No respect. No respect at all.

I'm disgusted. See?

Worried. What's in store? I look around and everything is breaking up. Everything's in pieces. These times we live in? What if something. Something really happened and everything. Who would look after us? Your mother and I are getting older and it seems everything could . . . destroy us. Nil? Nil? He won't look after us, his political mob would trample us. Or Teterev? Always sneering. People want to destroy our family. Beware of them, they want to destroy us all. And I feel it, all so close. This terrible . . . terrible disaster.

Pyotr Dad, really. Don't worry, my name'll be cleared and I'll go back and study.

Akulina Do it soon, Petya, for us.

Vassilly I believe you, Petya. When you're serious and sensible. That's how to live. All this mucking about upstairs / and time wasting.

Pyotr OK. Let's. Drop it.

Akulina Hug your dad.

Vassilly You should know they're / a bad mob.

Akulina Hug your dad.

Pyotr and Vassilly hug awkwardly.

Vassilly And then there's Tanya. Poor Tanya. Hopeless. Why doesn't she give up this teaching caper? All it does is make her tired.

Pyotr She needs a rest.

Akulina See if you can't talk to her about that, Petya,
sweet.

*Nil returns. Pyotr takes the opportunity at some point
to slip away unmolested.*

Nil Is dinner soon?

Vassilly Wash your face.

Nil That soon? I could eat a horse tonight. Big day: rain,
wind and cold. I'm tired. I'd love to see the boss handle
that filthy old engine in weather like this.

Vassilly Does the boss know your attitude towards him?
People are in positions of authority because they know
what's best.

Nil Best for me? Would be / him driving the engine.

Akulina Father means best for everybody.

Nil Everybody.

Vassilly Yes, everybody. So things can work the way
they're meant to.

Nil Things work the way it suits / the people in charge.

Vassilly Listen. You're not a fool.

Nil I'm listening.

Vassilly You're all a bit Mr Know-It-All.

Nil Since when?

Vassilly Where'd you get a tongue like that?

Nil I don't know.

He sticks it out provocatively at Vassilly.

You don't like it?

Akulina Put that away this / instant. Where does he –

Vassilly Mother, shut up. Go and help with the food.

Akulina leaves, containing her anger.

You listen to me –

Nil Later.

Vassilly Now.

Nil Can we eat first? What can you say to me? That you haven't already wittered on about? We argue and get nowhere. I don't / enjoy it. Neither do you.

Vassilly Have it your way, then.

And he storms off.

Nil See? A simple solution.
Boy, he's in fine form tonight.

Tanya Two hours we had of it.

Nil The never-ending Punch and Judy show.

Tanya It's all right for you.

Nil I get my fair share. Not for much longer, though. I'm moving to the depot; a position has come up as a fitter. I'm fed up of the goods trains. Long shifts, no one to talk to – I like people to talk to.

Tanya So . . . why leave?

Nil Here? I like people to talk to who are alive, thanks. I love noise and work. People at work are full of life, but here everyone just mopes around counting their money and moaning. Why?

Tanya Can't you see?

Nil Well, no. If it doesn't work? Fix it.

Tanya It has been said that life only seems simple to stupid people.

Nil Then I am stupid. / And what's the problem? At least I won't be bored by my over-intelligence.

Tanya I didn't say that.

Nil Actually, I think I might be smarter than you think. You complain, but who do you think will help you? No one will help you. I've worked that out.

Tanya Don't be too callous.

Nil Callous? *That's* callous.

He shows her his hand.

Tanya Now you sound like Teterev. Don't . . . I mean. Hating everyone, / that's hardly insight.

Nil He doesn't hate everyone. He's like an axe. Don't you think?

Tanya An axe?

Nil He just has this . . . axe-ish, well-worn . . . Tough. Dangerous. Useful. An axe.

Tanya He's all right, he's fine. He's a bit cruel. Anyway, you. You are. Fresh. Somehow . . . good. Nice to talk to. Except sometimes and then you can be . . .

Nil What?

Tanya Towards me you can be –

Nil What?

Tanya Sometimes very . . . overly . . . You can be hard. And I don't know . . . I'm.

Silence. Nil studies his boots. Tanya looks at him expectantly.

I'd love it if . . . I love it when. Sometimes.

45

Nil Thing is. With you . . . I . . . ?

Tanya is yearning for something.

You shouldn't teach, you know. You shouldn't teach,
because you don't like it. You don't like – people, really.
You don't like your students and they are young, they
will grow into the future, and you don't look after it.
You don't seem to want to help them.

You can't be good at anything if you don't love it. I love
working with metal. And, I know it: what it is. See? You
have this beautiful shapeless mass. Hot. Full of potential.
It's nothing at this stage, but if you work with it properly
it will be something. Something useful. See? But metal,
it's fierce too, burning hot, so you have to treat it with
respect. You have to approach it properly. It wants to
scorch your eyes, blind you, burn you. But that's because
it's alive. It's becoming something which is never easy. So,
you just have to knuckle in there and work at it, with it.
Towards what it can become. Not . . .

See? With it. Work with it.

Tanya Nil. Do you sometimes feel . . . ?
I don't know.

Nil What?

Tanya Sorry or . . . some . . . or –

Elena swirls in full of her next idea.

Elena Who's eaten? I've just baked the most fabulous
pie. Where's The Honourable Almost?

Nil Count me in. A fabulous pie! I could eat all of it.
They refuse to feed me here.

Elena It's your sharp tongue.

Nil News travels fast – who told you about my tongue
trick, then?

46

Elena Tanya? Shall we?

Tanya I'll. I should tell Mum.

She goes.

Nil So, this pie?

Elena I learnt to cook pies in jail. True story. One of my husband's prisoners taught me. He was a convicted murderer. Nice fellow, painfully thin.

Nil Your husband?

Elena No. Gawd. My husband was a fat little thing. Only this high, too.

Nil No . . .?

Elena Yes. Most impressive thing about him was his moustache. / Huge, hairy thing.

Nil I've never heard of anyone whose crowning achievement was their facial hair.

Elena I married a caterpillar, hoping for a butterfly.

Nil So, the killer pie?

Elena He was a cook. Had been. In the past. He killed his wife . . . but, you know, the way he tells it –

Nil She deserved it?

Elena The way he tells it.

Tanya stands in the door, watching them, Pyotr comes in at another door.

My One, my Only, Almost, my sweet. Come to dinner?

Nil / Elena has cooked a killer pie.

Pyotr That would be nice.

Elena Are you OK?

47

Nil He's had the old man at him all afternoon.
Will you be allowed to go to Elena's / room?

Pyotr Very funny.
Come on, then.

Tanya I'll –

Pyotr, Elena and Nil head away to Elena's room.
Tanya waits quietly. Akulina sneaks her head round
the door.

Akulina Tanya? Sweet?
So? Has Petya / gone?

Tanya I'm going too.

Akulina That's not very helpful, dear. She'll snare him.
She's got him in her clutches. You should be warning
him. Helping us. She's no match for your brother. She's
only three thousand roubles, you know. What does she
want, free rent? Free rent? Is that good / enough for your
brother?

Tanya / Jesus, Mum, leave it.

Akulina Don't blaspheme, dear.

Tanya (*simultaneously*) Elena is like that with everyone.

Akulina Exactly. She is. And she's playing him like a
professional. Stringing him along, make him jealous.
Build his. Fever. His –

Tanya Aagh. What do I care? Who cares? Tell him
yourself. Leave me out of it. Leave me. Be. Can't you see
how tired I am? How tired of all this? How tired and sick
and tired I am of all this? This.

Akulina Now, now, pet. You need a lie down and a relax.

Tanya Relax. How? Where? Here? With you in my ear?
I'm tired right down into here. All the way down into
here. For. Ever. Tired of you, of this, of everything.

She hurries out.

Akulina Heavens.

Vassilly comes in.

Vassilly What's her problem?

Akulina Nothing, dear. Nothing important.

Vassilly Was she rude? She's so bloody rude.

Akulina Leave her. It was nothing. Don't swear.
I said it was dinner and she said she wasn't hungry and
I worried that she wasn't eating and –

Vassilly Lies.

Akulina No, really, that was it. Just about dinner.

Vassilly Look me in the eye. See? Lies. They make you lie
to your own husband. What did we do? . . . See, Mum?
I can't. I don't.

They stand in silence. Sorrowful.

We did it to ourselves. They're from a different world
'cause of the schooling.

Akulina Enough, Father, anyone can be difficult. Not /
just educated ones.

Vassilly You should never give your kids more than you
have yourself. That's the truth of it. Family belongs in the
one spot, not all spread out teachers and lawyers. He
should have been a decorator like me. Taken over my
business. What is he? Who is he? I can't see them. I don't
know who they are, it's like they haven't any faces. No
character. Nothing strong in them, that distinguishes
them. Nil. I mean. He's a bugger / but he's got a face.

Akulina Dad.

Vassilly Excuse me.

49

When I was young I used to love singing in church.
I loved it. Singing in church and gathering mushrooms.
They were everything to me. But what does Pyotr love?

Akulina He's upstairs. With her.

Vassilly That. Little . . . I'll kill her. I'll kill her. I'll break
her –

Akulina She's got her claws in.

*Teterev barrels on, drunk as a lord, a bottle of vodka
in his hand.*

Vassilly God help us.

Teterev Been at it since yesters. Vesperday.
We eating?

Akulina I'll lay the table.

Vassilly You seem a clever man, why let the vodka
destroy you?

Teterev Venerable member of the bourgeoisie. It is not
the vodka that is destroying me.
It is me. My own strength. I've too much strength, you
see?

Vassilly I can't say that I do. You've only got yourself.

Teterev But there's a lot of me, you see?
These days? People that are true to themselves? Who can
only be themselves? People who are . . .? / These days . . .

Vassilly Strength never goes unrewarded.

Teterev Strength? Strength? No, no. You need cunning.
If I were to drive my fists into this cupboard. This
cupboard, for example? But what good would it do? See?
Or try and write? Put pen to paper and the nib bends
under my strength. The paper tears with every letter of
every word. There's no paper. No pen. All my strength?

Useless. Good for a freak show, bending iron bars for stunned ladies. I studied too. I can read and write and studied well enough to be kicked out by my teachers. Too strong in my opinions, you see? Too much again. Too much me. They want them quiet and polite. Unless they put you in a freak show. But that's not what I want. I want my audience worried, not amazed. I want them anxious, not curious. I want to break down from the stage and grab them up in my arms and crush the life out of them and wring them into – wring their . . .

Vassilly It's all right. It's all right. You. Settle down.

Teterev Settle down? No. Not for me. I don't want. I don't want a house. I'm better getting drunk and destroying myself than working for a house and place. People like you or some. Other type. Can you see me at some clerical? Bank? Well-groomed and dealing with all your queries most politely, sir. No.

Polya enters but, on seeing Teterev, spins to leave.

Please. Stay. I won't say anything, any more. Ever again.

He bows elaborately to her.

I am fully aware, Your Grace.

Polya What?

Akulina Polya? There you are. Go and help Stepanida with dinner, dear.

Vassilly Terenty, you don't need to be so angry, you know. You aren't a bad man at heart, are you?

Teterev I know what you're saying. I know what you mean. I like your cleverness, with just that exact amount of stupidity. You're a good man, but bad enough. Honest in a deceitful way. Scared when you need to be, but brave enough when things are going all right. You are

the definitional bourgeois man. The embodiment of
averageness, at the very plateau of banality. Banality,
which would drain the strength from Hercules. To you
the most common, humble, toothless shark, I . . . also . . .

He makes another wobbly bow.

Vassilly You want people to listen? Try not insulting them.

Nil enters.

Nil Is Polya back?

Teterev winks and smirks at him.

Akulina Why?

*Akulina looks between them. Nil is assessing how
drunk Teterev is. Teterev is swaying, winking and
smirking.*

Nil You're plastered?

Polya enters with Stepanida, carrying the food.

So? Polya?

*Polya tries to stop him asking – embarrassed,
indicating that this here, now, is not an ideal time.*

What? What's the matter?

Vassilly What's going on here?

Nil None of your business.

*Nil follows her to the table, where she is setting the
places with Stepanida.*

Polya?

Akulina I beg your pardon?

Vassilly What's going on here?

Teterev I know.

Vassilly Pelegaya?

Polya Nothing.

Nil Nothing? That's all? NOTHING?

He turns on Vassilly.

Keep out of it.
    Pelegaya? *Is* that your answer?

Vassilly What is this, some kind of secret club? This is
my house, I am master here, and I won't have secret
socialist codes going on over my dinner table. / What do
you think I am, an idiot?

Akulina Nil, really. Dad, don't let him . . .

Nil This is nothing to do with whether or not you're an
idiot. This is between Polya and I. Understand?

Polya Nil.

Nil What?
    It's nothing for him to get worked up over. It's none of
his business.

Vassilly It's my house.

Nil Listen –

Polya Nil. Yes. Yes. Nil. OK? YES.

Nil Yes?

Vassilly What?

Akulina What is all this, Pelegaya?

Polya It's not . . . Sir, ma'am? Nil, yesterday. Nil. Asked
me –

Vassilly What? WHAT?!

53

Nil Don't jump down her throat. I asked her to marry me.

Vassilly and Akulina are stunned.

I asked her yesterday and gave her till today to answer.

Teterev Simple.

Vassilly There you are, Mum, the future. Modern manners. There he is. / Modern gratitude and respect in one person. There.

Akulina Who do you think . . . ? The way you treat us? Doesn't even . . . Who are we, then?

Vassilly Leave it, Mother, it's not our business, just eat and be quiet. I'm going to be quiet in my own house. Just eat and try and keep my own things in order. In my own house. Our own house, Mother, we will just eat quietly and be quiet and shut our stupid mouths.

Teterev Well, I'm not going to. I'm going to. Say . . . ?

Quiet.

Vassilly That's my new policy. Just shutting up. Just letting them go to their hell in a basket. I'm not getting involved any more. But just to say, Nil. Just to warn you, Polya? This is Nil. This is him, *the great man* – with no gratitude. Not an ounce of any kind of decency. No thanks, no gratitude, no thanks for all our generosity. The time and help we have given / him over the years. *Years.*

Nil Generosity? I have paid for every *penny* of every *thing* you've *ever* given me. I've worked and paid my way and I keep doing it. But that doesn't mean, because you looked after me for a few years, that I / will do what you make me. Do . . .

Vassilly Is that all we did? That was it?

Nil You'd've married me to that old Sedovaya bag. For her dowry. No. No, I won't, I'll marry who I choose. I've loved Polya for years. It's no secret. There's no reason to be insulted.

Vassilly Insulted? I don't give a damn. I'm interested, though, to hear where you think you and your new wife will be living?

Nil I'm moving to the depot.

Vassilly / The depot?

Nil I'll pay you your thirty a month till the end of the year.

Vassilly End of the year.

Nil I pay my debts.

Vassilly Debts. I'll have that in writing, thanks.

Teterev Get it in writing. Exactly. End of the year. End / of the year.

Vassilly Shut up.
  End of the year? Three months' notice, is it? To terminate what? We have looked after you since you were ten. / Mother and I –

Nil Twelve.
  I've been working since I was fourteen. Paying you board.

Vassilly Board? I've fed you, sheltered you. I took you in and protected you. Put shoes on your feet. Food in your mouth.

Nil We can settle up later. Have you got the bill? Got it all in a ledger?

Teterev Every potato is / numbered. Individually.

Vassilly What if this is it, though, Nil? This behaviour? Have you thought of that. To act like this. Does this mean you and I are officially enemies? / I will not. I can't. I *must not*. I will *never* forgive this insult. *Never*.

Nil Insult? What *insult*? Were you expecting to marry me?

Akulina / Show some common –

Vassilly Mocking the person who fed you. Looked after you. Tried to guide you. Mockery. Without my permission. Did not ask my advice. And you? Young lady. / So submissive and quiet.

Nil Leave her out of this.

Vassilly All quiet are you, now? You know what I could do to you?

Nil You'll do nothing to her. What can you do? What can you do?
   Nothing. There is nothing you can do, you weak old man. *Nothing* you can do to us. Because? You are not the master here, any more. Money is the master in this house. You made money master in this house. Well, I've paid my way. I've worked and given you my pay for half my life. Money is the master here – in your life – and I've paid my way. There's a lot of me in here, too. My sweat. My work. When money is made the master, whoever pays can do what they like.

Teterev Money? Put a price on something, and suddenly it's worthless.

In the course of this outburst Polya leaves and Tanya and Pyotr return to the room.

Vassilly What? What's / he saying? He's the master?

Akulina Come on, Father. Come on, away. Out of here.

She is dragging Vassilly from the room, in the course of which she suddenly rounds on Nil.

56

You. You. Something. Something terrible. Just you wait.

Nil I didn't make money the master here.

Vassilly Calls himself / the master.

Akulina Come away, Father. No one is listening.

And they go. Nil is agitated. A barrel organ plays somewhere down the street.

Teterev Your classic Don Caesar. Just what Polya likes. We need more of it. The world is too full of these cunning villains. What we need now is more foolish heroes. / Fools and heroes – same thing.

Nil Where is she? Angry probably. / Fair enough.

Teterev Epiphany. The world as it currently stands – rotten and corrupted – is full of cleverness and cunning. So? It will take a fool to liberate us.

Nil This place disgusts me. Poor Polya, to have put her through it.

Teterev Fools, we need you. More fools, more idiots and wastrels. More spanners in the machine, bring down the whole rotten thing. More stupidity, that's what we need. More *stupidity*.

Nil Stupidity. That's me.

Teterev You? You are the stupidest fool of all.

Nil Yes. Sure.

Teterev To Jack Sprat and his perfect partner.

He drinks deep from the bottle.

Nil Shouldn't you go to your room?

Teterev What room? / My tomb? Not yet.

Nil To bed. I'll take you.

Teterev My room? Where's my room? There's no room for me. I am too big and awkward – too wild. There's no room here for me. No room anywhere for me.

Nil I can show you –

Teterev You can't show me. I show you. I am *the evidence*. I am the evidence of this crime. Life, Your Honour? Is ruined. Just look at me. It's a jumble, horribly sewn together. Sir. It cannot fit a decent person any more. The merchants and the painters – the money-grubbers – *sir*, have taken it in. Shortened it. Made it tighter. Cut some corners, saved some cloth. I'm the evidence – there is no room left.

Nil Come on.

Teterev Where?

Nil You're about to fall / over.

Teterev I can't fall. I can't fall any lower. I'm already down here. There's nowhere else lower I can go. I thought I might have a leg up and get onto doing something, but actually it was *you*. Of all people? You put in the final shove. No hard feelings. You didn't know I was already under. Go. I give you my love and my best wishes. Go.

Nil I don't understand.

Teterev What's to understand? Don't – for God's sake – understand. It's only agony and a waste of time. GO. Now, go, go. Fetch her. You must fetch Polya. Lovely . . .

Nil Yes. I will.

Nil leaves.

Teterev Good luck. Thief.

He notices Tanya.

Who's left?

Tanya Me.

The barrel organ stops.

Teterev I thought it was a ghost.

Tanya Me.

Teterev You too? Why are you left here?

Tanya I have nowhere. No place of my own to live, no means of my own to live. No reason of my own.

In the silence Teterev walks over to her slowly.

I'm sorry. To be so tired. I don't know why I am so tired and depressed. All the time. I'm ashamed, terribly, disgusted of feeling. Like this. Weak and . . . this emptiness. I'm all burnt out, dried up. I feel it. All.

It happened too slowly to stop. Imperceptibly. This empty hole in me. Sorry. I don't. Why I am telling you. It's . . .

Teterev I am very drunk. To understand. I don't . . .

Tanya No one talks to me how I want them too. I would like. And everybody fighting and. The crushing. Claustrophobia. I hoped he would. I waited quietly. I tried to hold on to . . . a thing, but I can't now. I haven't any strength. I even feel this . . . despair is watered. Away. Weak. I'm afraid. I'm very . . . suddenly very. Afraid. Of.

Polya hurries through, followed closely by Nil. Teterev moves off to the door, Tanya to the shadows.

Nil I'm sorry I handled that so badly. I just. I was desperate to know. I couldn't wait. I didn't even think.

Polya Not here, Nil. Don't. It doesn't matter. They'd never've been happy about it.

Nil You're so sweet. Why did you need till today?

Polya It seemed. To let it settle. I think I was too excited to speak anyway. Come on.

Nil Polya, wait. Feel it? This is it. Here. Stop here.

Our life is going to be wonderful, Polya. We'll start at the very bottom and climb the mountain together. I'll be with you always.

Polya I know. And I'll be with you.

Nil We're stubborn. And strong, you and I. Watch us, Polya. This will be wonderful. I am so happy. So . . . so happy.

Polya Me too.

Nil Life. This is life. To be alive.

Polya My sweet. Sweetest man.

Nil You, like this, now. This is the most beautiful thing. Just. You.

They kiss.

Polya Come on. We'd better go before –

Nil Who cares?

Polya Oh, but.
Kiss me again.

There is a shout off from Vassilly. 'Stepanida! Stepanida!' Polya breaks from the kiss and hurries away. Nil takes a deep, deeply satisfied breath. Then sees Tanya, watching greedily.

Nil What? Aagh . . . What? There's always somebody creeping around this place.

Nil goes and Tanya stands staring at the space where they were. Vassilly calls again offstage: 'Stepanida? Who spilled the coal?'
Blackout.

Act Three

The same room. Morning. Pyotr is standing aimlessly in the doorway of his room. Tanya hurries through to her room opposite. As she makes her way in, she looks to her brother. He rolls his eyes, bored, and drifts back into his bedroom. Tanya slips into her bedroom, clutching something. Stepanida and Akulina move through the room, cleaning.

Akulina Where did Tanya send you this morning?

Stepanida To the chemist. She had me buy liquid ammonia. Twenty / kopeks' worth.

Akulina She's always sick.

Stepanida She should get married.

Akulina We've tried. It's not easy, getting a girl married these days. Particularly if they've had a bit of education.

Stepanida Increase her dowry. A man'll only marry an educated girl if she's worth the trouble.

Pyotr is listening, unseen by the two women.

Akulina It's not the dowry, dear. It's Tanya, she just refuses the whole . . .

Stepanida Refuse all she likes, she's not getting any younger.

Akulina No.

Quiet.

Who visited our missy upstairs last night?

Stepanida The usual crowd. The teacher. The redhead.

Akulina The fellow whose wife ran off?

Stepanida Yes, him. And a new one, a man from the tax department. Thin fellow with yellowy skin.

Akulina Oh, yes. Married to Pimenov. It's consumption / does that.

Stepanida No doubt.

Akulina Teterev?

Stepanida Yes. Of course. Bawling out his songs. Two hours, he was, bellowing like an ox.

Akulina The usual, then.

Stepanida And Pyotr, too, you know?

Akulina And. When did he get back?

Stepanida It was light out when I let him in.

Akulina Light / out . . . ?

Pyotr Stepanida? Have you finished in here?

Stepanida I have. Just finishing up, sir. Yes.

Pyotr I'm sure you've got plenty of other things to be getting on with.

Stepanida exits.

Really, Mum. Do you think you should talk like that, about family . . . private. With the cook?

Akulina Who else is there? You don't talk to your / father and me.

Pyotr All you'll hear is gossip. Ignorant gossip.

Akulina It's better than nothing. You've been home a whole year. A whole year, and I haven't heard a word from you in that time. You haven't told me anything about Moscow. Anything.

Pyotr We've talked the whole / time.

Akulina We've argued. You've corrected me and mocked me. We've argued.

Pyotr is not in the mood. He walks away.

'Lovely talking to you, Mum.'

She goes back to her cleaning. Perchikin enters, looking like a ragbag.

Perchikin Are you all right? Petya's getting black as a crow. Not even a hello. What did he do? Have you seen Polya?

Akulina She's in the kitchen, chopping cabbages.

She sighs.

Perchikin Birds have it all worked out. When a chick has fledged, it's bye-bye. Skedaddle. None of your parental agonies. Would there be a little tea for an old fella?

Akulina Clearly you are following the birds' example.

Perchikin Whenever possible. I don't get in anyone's way, I've nothing. I live just a few feet above the earth.

Akulina You're a pest too, noisy, messy. There's your tea: cold and weak.

Perchikin A little on the empty side, but otherwise just the way I like it. I can see you might think me a pest. Most people are.

Akulina Have they been planning it long?

Perchikin Who?

Akulina What? Your daughter. Don't play the fool.

63

Perchikin She what?

Akulina Is getting married.

Perchikin When?

Akulina Don't. At your age.

Perchikin Hang on. Hang on. Stop. What is all this?

Akulina You've got no idea.

Perchikin What?

Akulina Your daughter. Pelegaya. Ungrateful and Nil. They're getting married.

Perchikin Nil? My daughter? Polya? My daughter? How fabulous. To Nil? Nil? And Polya? How fabulous. I thought he was going to marry Tanya.

Akulina Tanya? No thank you. Tanya?

Perchikin Lord, if I had ten daughters I'd let him have them all. Nil? That's a boy destined to be a man.

Akulina Well, that's going to be a lovely, happy little family. You both worshipping the great Nil.

Perchikin Me? No, they won't see me for dust. No one wants a father-in-law hanging around. No. Now I'm a free man. Now I can live . . . now I can just disappear into the woods.

Akulina Where will you go?

Perchikin I'll go and hunt the Fire Bird. I'm free. Free of all burdens. And even lighter – she's to marry Nil? So happy, healthy and . . . all that. Oh, I am the luckiest man alive today.

   Vassilly enters.

Vassilly Drunk again.

Perchikin Vassilly . . . I . . . ?

Vassilly Don't try that. Piss off.

Perchikin I wouldn't. You are . . . ?

Vassilly I said.

Perchikin OK. OK.
Goodbye, then.

Perchikin goes.

Akulina (*calling out*) Dad's here!

Pyotr enters.

How was –

Vassilly Have you collected that rent yet?

Pyotr I will, God. I will.

Vassilly It's part of your / obligations under the –

Pyotr I know. I know. For God's sake.

Pyotr leaves. Akulina is cleaning, muttering anxiously.

Vassilly What are you doing? Casting / a spell?

Akulina Praying. I'm praying, Father.

Vassilly Pray for the Jews.
I won't be Mayor. / After today.

Akulina Who said? What happened?

Vassilly Dosyekin? That . . . JEW . . . head of the metal workers' guild.

Akulina What's he want?

Vassilly He's teamed up with Filip Nazarov's son. /
They're just young men.

Akulina Is Nazarov a Jew?

65

Vassilly Nazarov? Probably. I'm not. We're not Jews. Well? No room for us any more in the new Russia. And that's my point. My point exactly. Dosyekin is in there at the Council . . . crapping on . . . how we all have to work together. Support one another. Build a new society. I say, to the Council generally . . . 'Excuse me, but it's the *Jews* are the problem here. Stick together?' I look around the room . . .? 'Stick together, all right. It's the Jews are taking over Russia in the first place. It's the Jews are corrupting our whole system. Get rid of the Jews and we will be getting somewhere.'

Nazarov can't hold my eye. Dosyekin's just smiling. Then Nazarov's son pipes up. 'And what of the Russians, who are more corrupt than the Jews? Do we get rid of them, too?' He's looking right at me. Then Dosyekin makes more speechifying and hints at this and that . . . and things I wouldn't have thought he'd be knowing about in the first place. Everyone's looking at me. I can see where he's heading. Council contracts. I'll get you, I'm thinking. I hiss at him, 'You cross-eyed Judas. You were prepared to profit.' He stings me then. Just disappears. Walks off . . .

Elena comes in.

Elena How are we all today?

Vassilly ignores her. Akulina stares at her like a disease.

Rent's due.

Vassilly Petya's collecting / that.

Elena I'd rather go straight / to the top.

Vassilly What have we owing, Mum? Twenty-five for / the room.

Elena Yes.

Vassilly Forty? Was it?

Akulina nods.

Forty for the windows. In the corridor. Your guests?

Elena Windows?

Vassilly The other was cracked. And the hinge on the door. / That was another twenty.

Elena I like accuracy in a man.

Vassilly Coal? And heating left on all day?

Elena Guilty.
So? What do I owe?

Vassilly Ninety-five.
Accuracy? Yes, madam. Accuracy is what is lacking in most human affairs, I find. The sun rises and sets accurately, has done for years. There is order in the heavens, we could do with more here on Earth. But you are prompt, at least. Always on time with your rent.

She hands him the money.

Elena I don't like to be in debt.

Vassilly Can't trust anyone who does.

Quiet.

Elena Well then, good evening to you. Both.

Vassilly And to you, madam.

Elena goes.

Good-looking bird, it has to be said.

Akulina Slut.

Vassilly Of course.

Akulina No shortage of tenants in the world.

Vassilly I'd be the first to toss her out.

Akulina Good idea.

Vassilly I will.
Except . . . if she goes? We might never see Petya. This way we can keep an eye on him. You know . . . she's always on time with her rent. Never queries the extras.
I just worry Petya would –

Akulina She is under our roof. He might just be . . . Maybe he just.
You know.

Vassilly Well, that's a point, Mother . . . if she's here. Paying rent. And keeping him. You know. Keeping him out of . . . brothels, lets / face it.

Akulina Father.

Vassilly Sorry, Mum. But it was . . .

A groan emanates from Tanya's room.

Akulina What's that?
Did it come from over there?

They listen for a beat.

I did want to say –

Vassilly What?

Akulina Were you a bit hard on Perchikin?

Vassilly I've had the garbage in this house up to here.

Another groan.

What is that?

Akulina I don't know.

Vassilly In here?

Tanya groans more loudly. She is offstage, in her room. They are in the doorway staring in. From within Tanya calls:

Tanya (*offstage*) Mama? Help me, Mama? Save me!

Vassilly and Akulina press into the room.

(*Offstage.*) My throat. Drink. Burning, Mama, please?

Akulina shoots back out of the room like a chook.

Akulina Oh God, oh God . . . / Help. Petya.

Vassilly (*offstage*) What have you . . .? My little girl?

Tanya (*offstage*) / I'm dying, I'm burning. Save me.

Akulina Help! In here. Help!

Pyotr runs on. As he does so Vassilly calls from within:

Vassilly (*offstage*) / Run, somebody. Call a doctor.

Pyotr What is it? What is it?

Akulina Tanya. Tanya. / Is dying.

Vassilly We need a doctor.

Pyotr (*simultaneously*) Let me go. / Let me see?

Teterev appears.

Teterev / Tanya?

Vassilly A doctor, call a doctor.

Vassilly's hands are filled with Elena's rent. Pyotr cranes past him into Tanya's room, where she is groaning.

Pyotr. Here's money. Anything. That's ninety. / Offer him twenty-five to start.

Pyotr is taking the money from Vassilly, who is trying to count it.

Teterev What's she done?

Pyotr Liquid ammonia. Swallowed. Tell him a girl swallowed liquid ammonia.

Teterev takes the money from Pyotr and hurries out. Stepanida rushes in.

/ Hurry. Quickly. Hurry.

Vassilly Twenty-five roubles, should do it.

Stepanida (*simultaneously*) What's happened? What's happened?

Vassilly is hovering in the doorway. Pyotr is back in Tanya's room, talking offstage to her:

Pyotr (*offstage*) / What did you do? When did you take it? How much? *Tell* me.

Tanya (*offstage*) I'm burning. I'm burning. I want to live. Please. Sorry.

Stepanida (*simultaneously*) What happened? Oh my goodness, my goodness.

Vassilly (*simultaneously*) My little darling girl.

Akulina (*simultaneously*) She's destroyed herself. Our darling girl. Destroyed herself.

Pyotr shoots his head back into the room. Elena comes in from upstairs.

Pyotr Shut up. All of you. Go away. Elena, get them out of here.

An Old Crone pokes her head in the door from the street. Pyotr returns to Tanya's groanings. Vassilly pushes his way back into Tanya's room, out of his depth. Elena bundles up Akulina carefully:

Elena / It'll be all right. It's not dangerous.

Akulina What did I do? What did I do?

Elena These things pass. / Nothing. It'll be nothing.

Akulina My sweet. My darling . . . What can I do?

They get Akulina out of the room to the kitchen. The stage is briefly empty. We hear Tanya's groans and Pyotr's earnest, quiet questioning tone, punctuated by Vassilly: 'Where's the doctor?', 'What did we do?' Crockery clatters in the kitchen. A chair falls and the groans escalate from Tanya's room. Stepanida runs madly from kitchen to street to Tanya's room trying to be helpful. Increasingly dishevelled. From off there is clearly a crowd gathering at the street door. A young man pokes his head in boldly. He turns back to the crowd just pressing in offstage: 'She's dead, I'd say.' Others mutter and speculate. 'Was it the father?', 'Beat her head', 'No? Really?', 'She slit her throat, I hear', 'What about her husband?' Much muttering and surprise: 'She isn't married? Well . . .' Etc. The Old Crone comes back out from the kitchen and steals a loaf of bread from the table. She looks back at the crowd pressing in at the door.

Old Crone What? We need quiet. That's what they need. / Go away. Go.

Man's Voice What's her name then?

Old Crone Lizavetta.

Woman's Voice Why'd she do it to herself?

Old Crone Ascension Day last there was a big to-do. People have said all . . .

Teterev pushes through with a Doctor. The Doctor goes straight to the room. Teterev looks in briefly, then moves away. He looks at the crowd.

Teterev Go away. It's none of your business. This is not . . .

Voices and groans come from Tanya's room, from another Akulina is heard crying and wailing. From the street door, the murmur of gossip and morbid fascination. Teterev crosses to the street door.

What do you all want? Go.

Old Crone The man is right. On / your way.

Teterev Who are you?

Old Crone I sell vegetables.

Teterev What are you doing here?

Old Crone I was on my way to Semyagina's. She's godmother / to my children.

Teterev So what are you doing here?

Old Crone Helping. Helping. I thought there was a fire.

Teterev There is no fire. Get out. Everyone get out. Get moving. This is not. Sport. This is not. For you. GO.

Stepanida shoots from Tanya's room. An Old Man sticks his head in and collars Teterev.

Stepanida / Water they need now. Water.

Old Man She stole a loaf of bread.

Old Crone I did not.

Teterev Out, all of you. OUT!

Pyotr sticks his head out.

Pyotr QUIET! Please.

Pyotr looks back into the room, disappearing to his sister as he talks.

(*Offstage.*) Dad, go. Go to Mum. (*He calls back.*)
Terenty, keep them away please? Go, Dad. Go to Mum.

*Vassilly comes from Tanya's room. Swaying. He takes
a seat. From the other room Akulina's sobs and
mutterings rise up as Stepanida hurries out with water.
She crosses back to Tanya's room. Vassilly is seated,
holding his head in his hands. Akulina appears in the
door of the kitchen, eyes popping with anxiety.*

Akulina Didn't I love her? Didn't I try and keep her
happy?

Elena Calm down. There's nothing you can do out there.
Stay here.

Akulina I need to be helpful. I can get water. I can get
water.

*Vassilly stands and crosses to his wife at the door. As
he goes in we hear:*

(*Offstage.*) Father. Father? What have we done?

Elena (*offstage*) Shh. Now shh. Here he is.

The door shuts. Stepanida appears from Tanya's room.

Teterev Well?

Stepanida It's all right.

Teterev The doctor said that?

Stepanida Yes. The doctor. And. They don't want. Them,
to go in. Just now.

Teterev Is she better?

Stepanida She's not groaning. She's very green. Eyes
like . . . huge – They've got her lying down.
I said to them. I said it time and again. She needs to
be married.

Teterev Don't crow.

Elena slips out of the other room, which has also settled into quiet sobbing.

Elena How is she?

Teterev She'll be all right, apparently.

Elena They won't. Poor things. They're beside themselves.

Stepanida The cabbage soup.

Stepanida hurries out to the kitchen.

Elena Sounded like she was in agony. Is it agony, do you think?

Teterev I couldn't say. I've never drunk liquid / ammonia.

Elena Don't joke.

Teterev I'm not.

Elena And. Pyotr? He's – Is he still with her?

Teterev I haven't seen him come out.

Elena This'll get to him. His sister.
When I see this sort of thing. I'm torn and I . . . I hate people's. Problems.

Teterev Very noble.

Elena I do. I just want to grab them out of it. And I want to trample on problems. Get rid of them. Break them all for ever.

Teterev What would be left?

Elena I detest them. I hate the . . . mess of people's –
I like being happy. What's wrong with that? Enjoying life, meeting people. Find ways to make life interesting and fun for myself and my friends. The people I love.

Teterev You seem to love. Everybody.

Elena No. No, I can be callous. This. I can be harsh. Stuff like this? I won't lie to you. / I don't like. Unlucky . . .

Teterev No, don't.
Go on.

Elena There's a type of person seems to bring it on themselves. You take their hat off them so they can enjoy a bit of sun and all they do is whinge about getting burnt. And how alone they are and how dark and pointless life is and I just – Those people, I can't help myself, I want them to be unhappy. I just. Do.

Teterev Well, fancy that.
If we're confessing? Usually? When women try and understand something, I just switch off, but you? I want to kiss your hands.

Elena Only my hands? I'll have to try and understand things more often. No, no. We shouldn't be so flippant when someone is suffering.

Teterev Someone's always suffering.

Elena I do feel for her.

Teterev So do I.

Elena I pity her . . . and.

Teterev It's better to help someone than pity them.

Elena You can't help everyone. You're more likely to help someone if you feel something for them. Pity . . . ?

Teterev Suffering? Springs from one place: desire. There are desires that are noble and good and desires that are rotten and mean. We should only help someone satisfy their good desires. The ones which will make them healthy and strong. Raise them above the animals they basically are.

Elena Mmm.

It's weird, suddenly there is noise and disaster. Then just as quickly silence and stillness.

Teterev Life. People shout, fight, eat and go to bed. When they wake up? They start shouting again. In this house everything fades quickly. Tears, laughter. Everything. Dissipates. The last sounds ringing out over a lake. Then nothing. A banal hum. The banal hum is the underlying sound. That's the final sound round here – a banal hum.

Elena We are – none of us – are free here. My last life was very different. Prison, you know. Very interesting. Prison, and I was free – my husband was a terrible gambler. And when he wasn't gambling he was hunting with the other wardens. Hunting and gambling and beer. Hunting, gambling, beer. Gambling, hunting, gambling and BEER.

I didn't mind. I was free. I didn't have to go anywhere, didn't know anyone. Only the prisoners. They loved me, those men. Once you got to know them . . . they were quite mad, yes. But sweet, mostly, and simple. After a while, I didn't think they were murderers and thieves and oh . . . you name it. Sometimes it would come up, and I would be, 'Did you really kill someone?' 'Yes, I killed someone, Elena Nikolaevna. I did. But what can you do?' And somehow, in a funny way it seemed to me these men had regained a kind of innocence. They had . . . Or in a way, we all have a share in the guilt? Kind of abstractly: they were . . . what? Stones? That chance . . . That something . . . life. Had thrown. Yes . . . And that can be? Life can. Take over. Choice is not so simple. So far-reaching.

I bought them books, draughts, cards. Little things. Sometimes tobacco, even a bit of vodka when my husband was away. In the exercise yard they played bowls. They loved it, like children. You know, the way children play? I would read to them, most of them couldn't read. I'd read, funny stories, short stories. They loved to laugh. You know, for the most part. Enjoying whatever was left, you see? I bought little birds. I'd try and find them each a bird that seemed to suit them. In a cage. There were a lot of bullfinches and canaries. Not that many doves, it has to be said, but then not that many crows either.

And dressing was fun, because they appreciated what I wore. If I wore a bit of colour they'd go all wide-eyed. Colour. Colour. It was wonderful, living there. Three years passed in a flash. When my husband was killed in the hunting accident? I wept. Oh God, I wept, but not for him. No, the amount of things he'd killed or tried to kill. It seemed like some kind of justice, really. No, I was sad to go. And the prisoners. They were sad.

But I had a town, a new town, not a prison to look forward to, another life. I'd been thrown another life. But . . .

And then I think about here. This place. This is worse, far worse. Ooh, yuck. I'm getting all bleah. Yuck, and here we are chatting away while someone might be dying in the next room.

Teterev It's because we don't feel sorry for them.

Elena You don't?

Teterev Neither do you.

Elena I know, it's bad. I'm trying. I'm trying, but I keep thinking she sort of brings it . . . I feel worse for Pyotr. You know . . .? He . . . I feel bad for him here. It's bad for him here, isn't it?

Teterev It's bad for everyone here.

Polya enters.

Polya Hello –

Elena Shh. We're being quiet. Tanya. Tried to poison herself.

Polya What?

Elena The Doctor's with her, and Pyotr.

Polya Is she . . . ? Will she . . . ?

Elena Who knows?

Polya Did she say? Why? Did she / say anything?

Elena I don't know. No.

Pyotr appears in the doorway of Tanya's room.

Pyotr Elena? Could you . . . ?

Elena hurries over, and she and Pyotr return to the sickroom. Silence.

Polya What?

Teterev What?

Polya You've always got this look. It's not my fault.

Teterev I didn't say a –

Polya You didn't have to. What happened? How / did she . . . ?

Teterev Yesterday? She was nudged. And today? She fell over.

Polya Rubbish.

Teterev What?

Polya I know what you're saying. It's nothing to do with Nil and me.

Teterev She –

Polya Neither of us. I know you're thinking us, but . . . It's not. I love him. He loves me. / It started a long time ago.

Teterev Face it or it will eat you. I'm not blaming you, but you will blame you. And that is the problem with this place . . . These people? I told you to get away. Away from.

Polya Well, I will . . . Away. I / will, but . . .

Teterev All along I said get away. And this would not have happened to you. To you and Nil. You'd be gone . . . see?

Polya What's she done? Is it bad? What . . . ?

Teterev It doesn't matter. This is the bad bit. For you. What's bad for Tanya is what is bad for Tanya. And . . .

Pyotr and the Doctor come from Tanya's room.

Pyotr Polya, can you . . . help Elena?

Teterev So?

Doctor It'll be fine. She's very nervy, which makes her . . . unpredictable but it isn't serious. She only drank a little. Burnt her oesophagus, that's about all.

Pyotr Doctor, have a seat.

Doctor She'll need to rest for a week or so. Then it's a question of keeping her stable. Not too. Fraught. I had one last week. A decorator, drank a glass full of varnish. Thought it was beer.

Vassilly appears in the doorway to the kitchen.

Pyotr It's . . . Don't worry, OK? Don't. It's not as bad as it –

Doctor Physically? She'll be on her feet in a week at the most.

Vassilly That's all?

Doctor Physically, yes.

Vassilly That's good. Very good. Thank you. Pyotr?

Pyotr goes to his father, who is whispering something to him about money and Teterev. Teterev over the course of the next interchange, realising what Pyotr and Vassilly are discussing, begins rather ostentatiously to play with Elena's rent money.

Teterev What happened to that decorator?

Doctor Sorry?

Teterev The varnish?

Doctor Ah . . . yes. Nothing. He recovered. Do I know you?

Teterev Don't you?

Doctor Were you? In hospital with typhoid?

Teterev I was.

Doctor I never forget a / face. Spring.

Teterev I remember you.

Doctor You do?

Teterev I was just getting better. Getting my appetite back – very hungry, and you said, 'Don't expect more. You're lucky to have been seen to, there's no shortage of drunks in the world.'

Doctor Is that . . . ? Did I? Your name? I'm Dr Troerukov.

Teterev I am the drunkard. Guardian of the Green Genie. And your paymaster. I won't bite.

He hands him the wad of cash and, with a wink to Vassilly, he goes.

Vassilly I think we settled on twenty-five? Pyotr.

Pyotr Sorry, Doctor.

Doctor Yes, OK.

Vassilly Twenty-five. We decided. Sixty-five change.

Doctor Yes. Yes. Well, if she complains about the pain. Um. You know, give her another drop. It should be fine. I'd better be off. Your brother is a . . . / very original –

Pyotr No. He's a lodger.

Doctor Aah. Anyway. Yes. OK. Great.

Pyotr shows the Doctor out. Vassilly intercepts the remainder of the rent as they leave. Akulina appears in the kitchen doorway and heads over to Tanya's room. Vassilly stops her.

Vassilly Wait. Don't. Just yet. She might be sleeping. Oh, Mother, I hate today. Gossip'll be all over town by now.

Akulina It doesn't matter – she's alive, Father.

Vassilly Yes, yes of course. But you know. What a day. With the Council.

Akulina What can they say?

Vassilly That we are to blame. That we upset her. As if we treat them badly? That'll be the word. Unmarried daughter who attempts to . . . (*A*) Son in trouble with the State. Stepson bloody (*B*) socialist runs off with the maid. Can't even hold a household together. (*C*) That's the gossip. That'll be the talk. Well. Damn them, the Jews and the gossips. They don't know what we . . . I don't understand. I don't understand your children. Why are they so weird?

Akulina (*overlapping at A*) Now.
  (*Overlapping at B.*) Dad.
  (*Overlapping at C.*) That's not how . . .

I know, Dad, and it hurts me, too. I try everything I can. All day and never a thank you. But what can we do? They are alive and healthy.

Vassilly Yes, but . . . What? What? What?

Polya appears from the room.

Polya Shh. She's asleep.

Vassilly How does she look?

Akulina Can I go in? I'll be very quiet. Father / and I –

Polya The Doctor said. Not to let anyone in, just now.

Vassilly Why are you in the know?

Polya Elena asked me.

Vassilly Why's she allowed in? Strangers? But not her / own flesh and . . .

Akulina Father. We should have some soup. So's not to disturb her. We'd better. I'd love to have a peek. But, come on. Eat.

She drifts back through to the kitchen. Vassilly does not follow.

Vassilly Happy now?

Polya leaves and, thinking the coast is clear, Vassilly tries to sneak into Tanya's room. Elena comes out, stopping him.

Elena What are you doing? Shh. She's asleep, don't disturb her.

Vassilly Oh yes. But she can do whatever she likes, can she? And disturb us?

Elena Don't be ridiculous. She's unhappy.

Vassilly Why?

Elena Shh. Leave her be.

Vassilly gives in and retreats to the kitchen.
Elena walks around the room, enjoying the quiet.
Pyotr appears from the street door.

Petya?

Pyotr Yes.

Elena I feel sorry for you. In all this.

Pyotr I feel sorry enough for myself.

Elena You should go away.

Pyotr Yes.

Elena What do you want . . . from life? Tell me?

Pyotr Things change. I can't really say.

Elena Even to me?

Pyotr Especially to you. I worry. How can I know what you think of me or what I might really think? My opinions?

Elena Try me.

Pyotr I can't.

Elena I think you are wonderful. Will it change that?

Pyotr What is wonderful about me? You all think I'm a coward and egotist. Maybe I am.

Elena I don't think that.

Pyotr Well, Nil and Shyshkin and Tsvetaeva do, and they are your friends. The chorister who you are always flirting with. That's what they think. That's what they say, because I've changed. I've stopped seeing the world the way they do. You think I am a coward for that?

All I see? Here? Is a waste of good people. No one's going to look after us. No one can. No one will love Tanya the way she wants. It's not possible. I've seen the way the world works. It's every man for himself. You

83

can't change soldiers, and what if you could? They're only going to be shot for their new opinions. I'm sorry. And I should be better than this, than I am here, in this house. This house, this place it just . . . sucks the –

I have more. In me. I've got more I can do. Wasting my time trying to help everybody. Nothing comes of it, you can only look after yourself. I ran down the alley during that demonstration. And when we hit that wall? There weren't noble sentiments of people giving each other a leg up, mark my words. You just . . .

They looked out. You looked out for yourself. Sorry. I'm sorry, but I've seen it. Finally all that sentiment and nicety is a waste of time. And I don't want to say it to you because you probably think everyone should be good to each other. Or . . .? Sure. I mean, sure. But it isn't like that. And if I miss my time, trying to help everyone? If I get all caught up as an 'Almost'? No one will actually care. Nothing will be any better. And my life will be gone . . . I'm sorry, but that's what I think.

And I just want to . . . Get on with my stuff. And . . .

Elena You're tired.

Pyotr No. I'm angry. And.
I have the right to live how I like. How I like.

Elena I live how I can. I do what I want. I'm not interested in being a nun. I don't want to pick fruit. I'd rather be dead.

Pyotr You're always with them. Nil and Shyshkin. Terenty. You like them more than me. But they are . . . They don't know. They are wrong.

Elena They do what they want. I like them because they are full of life and activity.
If they are wrong? Am I?

Pyotr You're different. You are. Life. A mountain stream.

Elena Cold?

84

Pyotr Don't. What is so funny? Am I an idiot? I'm not an idiot. I want to live. I want to live my own life. To the full.

Elena What's stopping you?

Pyotr Something. Something nags at me. Niggles at me. Just when I am finding my feet. Pulls me down.

Elena Your conscience?

Pyotr Conscience? Why? No. I just want to live. And make my decisions and lead my life. And –

Elena What? Try saying something exact that you want. I can help you.

Pyotr Elena. Don't joke and tease me. It's torture. I mean, I am here. Begging you.

Elena Is that all you wanted to say to me?

Pyotr I'm weak and unsure. But I know what . . . I know I just. I need to get away and live alone and do more exercise. And. You know, become . . . I know all the things . . .

Elena Was that it?

Pyotr What?

Elena What you wanted to say to me?

Pyotr I will. I do know.

Elena Repeat after me: I. Love. You.

Pyotr Very funny.

Elena No. Very serious.
  I want to marry you. It might not work but it's what I want.

Pyotr That's . . . Are you? Don't. Elena? Really. I'm so . . . I'd love you like. I do. I love you.

Tanya groans from her room. The two stop, Pyotr as if he had just seen a ghost, Elena cool as a cucumber.

Is that Tanya? Sorry, that's. We can't.

Elena There's nothing wrong. / We can be happy.

Tanya (*offstage*) Water? Drink. Something. Please.

Elena I'll get it.

Elena heads out to the bathroom. Pyotr stands, anxious and excited. Akulina pokes her nose in.

Akulina Petya? Are you in there too?

Pyotr Here. Yes. Me?

Akulina Come in and have something to eat, there's a good lad.

Pyotr I'm. I'm OK, thanks. Just –

Elena returns with a glass of water.

Elena He'll eat with me tonight.

Elena crosses to Tanya's room and slips in with the water. Akulina stands, staring.

Pyotr I will. Tonight. I will, yes.

Akulina retires to the kitchen. Elena comes out from Tanya's room.

It's wrong. She's sick in there. And Mum and Dad.

Elena Let's go. It's not wrong. It's life.

Pyotr presses himself against her. She takes his hand and leads him away.

Tanya (*offstage*) Lena? Lena? Someone?

Tanya wanders in.
Blackout.

86

Act Four

The same. Evening.
   A sudden burst of laughter. Tanya is lying on a couch in the corner. Tsvetaeva and Shyshkin are around her, readying to leave. Polya is laying out the things for tea.

Shyshkin Exactly, exactly. We have to.

Tanya You must, you must. Now please. Go. Go, now.

Tsvetaeva Yes, yes. Goodbye, Tanya. Tomorrow's Sunday. I'll pop by in the morning. You look / much better.

Tanya That will be. That will be good. Yes. Now, go. Both of you go and . . .
   I feel like some kind of creeper or weed dragging and clinging at people's feet.

Shyshkin No. No, now what good / is that, then?

Tsvetaeva Tanya, don't. It hurts us to hear you talk like that.

Tanya I can see you both, your belief? Your belief, belief – you see? Helps you through. Evolution of the species, demands the ability to be deluded, to have belief. That's how / we carry on.

   Simultaneously Shyshkin laughs hard over the top of Tanya.

Shyshkin Genius! Now there's a theory.

Tsvetaeva Are you making fun of us?

Tanya I am deadly serious. Don't laugh at me.

Shyshkin / I'm not . . . no . . .

Tsvetaeva Now it's just – Tanya? That's just your exhaustion talking.

Tanya Go, both of you. Go. And goodbye. Goodbye.

Shyshkin (*to Polya*) You need to read Heine. Even a married . . . anyway. Yes. Well, whatever. Goodbye.

Shyshkin and Tsvetaeva exit. There is a long cool silence as Polya fusses with things for and around Tanya. Eventually:

Polya Vespers will probably be over soon . . . I'll get the samovar on.

More silence.

Tanya I used to find the silence here oppressive, but now I crave it.

Polya Is it time to take your medicine?

Tanya Shyshkin is so noisy.

Polya He has a good heart.

Tanya Like all idiots.

Polya Well then, idiots are smart. Enough . . . to stick by what they believe. He knows how people live. The servant, for instance, he was talking about? Who else would notice that and do something about it?

Tanya Are you anxious? Marrying Nil? / Worried?

Polya What . . . should I be . . .? No.

Tanya I would be. I'm only . . . I love you, Polya, and I want you to know . . . You're not the same as him. He's read a lot. He's educated. I taught him to read. He might soon get bored of you. Have you thought what that. Means?

Polya No. Love is . . . I know he loves / me.

Tanya How can you know that? People talk. They can say anything. A word is easy. An unwitting lie. Is easy.

Teterev brings on the samovar.

Polya We'll need milk.

Polya goes.

Teterev Stepanida begged me. She offered me endless pickles. 'It's too heavy . . . It's too heavy.'

Tanya Have Vespers finished?

Teterev I didn't get there. Head.
  How are you? Today?

Tanya Fine. The noise and carry on. That's what annoys me. Everyone's always so busy. Stupid insects.

Teterev It can be interesting.

Tanya When? This mess?

Teterev In its own way. Before a concert? When the musicians are tuning up their instruments? Warming up. Think of it like that. You can hear fragments, distinct little pieces. A trumpet suddenly. Violins . . . every now and then a lovely phrase. And in all that disorder you begin to look for the tune. What will they play when they settle into it? Those moments it's as if I hear people tuning up for their life.

Tanya Waiting for the conductor to come along and whip them into shape? Play some tired old piece of pompous rubbish. Miss the beat, drag on all the changes. Lovely.
  What could they play, though? These people? Of interest?

Teterev Something loud.

Tanya Mmhhhm.

Teterev lights up his pipe. Tanya watches.

Is the pipe an affectation?

Teterev It lends the tramp an aura of mystery. A hauntingly noble past.
　　I'll hit the road again soon.

Tanya Where?

Teterev Doesn't matter.

Tanya You'll freeze to death somewhere. Drunk on the roadside.

Teterev I never drink on the roadside. And so what? It's better to freeze to death on the move than rot in the one place.

Tanya Rotting, am I?

Teterev No. I didn't mean. I wasn't. I wouldn't.

Tanya I don't care. I don't care about anything. Nothing hurts. Nothing hurts me.
　　In fact it's all the politeness and niceness that. Disgusts. Most. I know how the beggar feels at the church door. So nice and generous of all you healthy, happy folk to deign to be so sweet and kind to poor me.

Teterev You're very hard. Relentless with / yourself.

Tanya Shut up.
　　Relentless? What about you? Drunk all the time? Wandering around? That's hard. On you.
　　Tell me? Who are you?

Teterev That's a big subject. And dull. Like Geography.

Tanya Perfect. Go on. Why? Why are you so hard on yourself?

Teterev If I had words. What would I say? . . .

Everyone is flawed. That's why our hearts go out to each other.

Learn to live with your flaw. Honestly. And the better your chances of being loved. Properly loved . . .

But that is not even pat enough. For a drunk it's acceptable to be sentimental. More acceptable than a hard-working, honest person.

Nil and Pyotr arrive.

Tanya Nil? Where have you been?

Nil At the depot. I just walked all over that idiot manager.

Pyotr Who's now working out the best way to sack you.

Nil I'll work / somewhere else.

Tanya Speaking of which? Shyshkin was here, apparently he had a fight with Prokhorov, and Prokhorov doesn't want him as a tutor any more.

Pyotr Bloody hell. What did they have to fight about? We lose Prokhorov . . . Did you explain to him that's one less convert to his noble cause?

Nil Well, maybe it was fair enough.

Pyotr No. Shyshkin is too hot-headed.

Tanya Apparently Prokhorov is anti-Semitic.

Pyotr Yes. A bit.

Nil Well. Good on Shyshkin / then.

Pyotr No. I mean, exactly, of course you would say that, but really? Surely people are entitled to their opinions.

Nil Opinions that are worth respecting yes, but anti-Semitism is garbage.

Pyotr All I'm saying? You can't just jump down someone's throat.

Nil Sometimes you should.

Teterev opens his mouth and gurgles an 'aaaah', by way of invitation.

Pyotr No. You can't just –

Nil Sorry, but you have to. You have to go on the front foot or be crushed by the weight of ignorance.

Pyotr / Oh Jesus, help us.

Tanya Rubbish. I can't believe it. We are here again. You / two are . . .

Pyotr All right. All right. Sorry. Shh. I just. But you know Shyshkin can be such a . . .

Tanya Yes. That's why we love him.

Nil No. He's got beliefs and he sticks by them. That is a virtue.

Tanya Unless his beliefs don't concur with yours. What if Shyshkin was the anti-Semite?

Nil He's not.

Tanya Nil? You really are . . .

Nil What? This is ridiculous. He's not / an anti-Semite.

Pyotr Shut up. I got him that work . . .

Nil Should he just do what he is told – is that what you're . . .?

Pyotr If he needed the work badly enough? He would, sorry.

Nil No. He has the guts. He has the belief. He will bite the hand that feeds him if he senses it is also the hand that beats him.

Pyotr Yes. But that's pretty slippery. Ethically.

Nil What?

Pyotr Not that Father ever beat you. But I'm sure you've convinced / yourself otherwise.

Nil What are you going on about?

Pyotr / Biting the hand that feeds you.

Teterev Children! Children, please!

Nil You are defending the old man? Your father? Everything he does and says disgusts me.

Pyotr Sometimes I agree with you. But you still take his / hospitality.

Nil I pay for it, thank you.

Pyotr But if he disgusts you, why are you still here?

Nil What?

Pyotr And your constant attacking of him and winding him up? It leaves Tanya and I in the – All the time. We are trying to find / another way . . .

Nil You are trying to find? What?

Tanya Enough. All of you. Enough. I am officially . . . BORED.

Polya enters, carrying a pitcher of milk.

Tanya Look how happy she is.

Nil She has spirit.

Pyotr Born blind, was she?

Tanya A good argument / for it.

Nil She likes living. Is that so bad? I like living. It is a great pleasure to live on this Earth.

Teterev Certainly passes the time.

Pyotr Stuck here? Waiting for what?

Nil You? You amaze me. I mean, we all know you are in love and. *And*. Which is very rare round here – you are *loved* in return. And yet? I don't see a shred of happiness. Why / aren't you singing and dancing?

Pyotr That'd be great except. *Except* . . . I can't as a student – afford to get married. And then they would . . .

Nil Run away.

Tanya He's just saying, Nil. Life? This thing? It might actually be complicated. It can still be hard and painful, even when it is perfect and wonderful and beautiful and lovely.

Nil I know. I know it's not easy. I know when things aren't easy, but even so. I've worked straight shifts on those trains in the freezing cold for . . . for. Arseholes. But still it can be amazing. Still life is amazing.

Pyotr Maybe when you hit a brick wall, we'll see what you say.

Nil I know what I'll say, because I will grip life by the throat and make it say what I want to hear. I will smash through whatever brick wall to make life into the thing that I can see. That I want.

Teterev There we are. Who needs philosophy when you have brute strength?

Elena trots in.

Elena Another wrestling match? World Championship Philosophy?

Nil I was singing the hymn of life. Life is a pleasure.

Polya Life is a joy.

Elena Certainly.

Nil gathers Polya up to him for a kiss.

Heavens. Sweet and sour as ever. Can you stop that?

Pyotr Nil, are you drunk?

Tanya moves away and slumps onto the sofa.

Elena It's cheerful here today. I might have tea down here. Unless you all want to come upstairs? Terenty, you can smile.

Teterev I'm happy. I keep happiness to myself. It's misery I shout about.

Nil Shout it from the mountain tops. Misery Be Damned.

Elena Did you know, Tanya? He's teaching me philosophy. Yesterday we began with the Law of Sufficient Reason. How do you describe it again?

Teterev Nothing exists without reason, because / it is . . .

Elena That's it. Teeth. Teeth have four roots. Which also . . .

She waves her hand philosophically aloft.

Teterev Very wise. Very wise. Pray continue.

Elena One of the roots. On the tooth of knowledge. The first? Maybe not. But one of these roots of this tooth of understanding is the Law of Sufficient Reason of Being. 'Being' being matter in form. I, for instance, am the matter which is – rather conveniently for me – in the form of a woman.

Teterev And what a woman.

Elena But then – and this is the complicated bit – I am in one way devoid of being. Being is eternal but matter in form – which is the bit that is here right now – exists for

a time on Earth and then disappears while the other bit.
Is eternal?

Teterev Kind of.

Elena There's also a causal bit. *A priori* or *a posteriori*
or . . . I've forgotten how that links. I can see, however,
just in one educative flurry how thinking makes you
frown.

Teterev I always thought it was frowning that made me
think.

Elena And we always thought he was thinking. But that
is the really useful thing about philosophy. Why, Terenty,
does a man talk philosophy with a woman?

Teterev Because it increases the length of time he gets to
look at her.

Elena See? See? And why, Terenty, does she let him?

Teterev When a man philosophises he does not lie.
Because no one is listening.

Elena Thus it may be useless – but it serves the greater
purpose. The continuation of the species.

Teterev If nothing else.

Elena I'm desperate to have a sing.

Pyotr Perhaps we should wait till Vespers is over.

Vassilly and Akulina enter in their Sunday best.

Elena Vespers is. Worshippers, good day.

Vassilly and Akulina nod cursorily.

So . . . was it hot in church?

Vassilly We didn't go there to take the temperature.

96

Elena No, of course. What I meant was . . . Was it crowded?

Akulina We didn't count.

Vassilly Do people still go, do you mean? Yes, a lot of people still go. Most people still go to pay their respects to the Lord. Most.

Polya Tea?

Vassilly Supper first. Mother, go and get the food ready.

Akulina exits. In the quiet people rearrange themselves. From nowhere:

People have become such thieves.

On our way to church this morning. Mother and I. To get over a muddy patch on the path. I put down an old plank, so we could walk over it. We got back this afternoon? Gone.

Life . . .? Nowadays. Life is brimming over with corruption.

Thievery was not as petty in the past. People stole on a grander scale and this is because they had bigger hearts and souls. Bigger lives. A plank of wood? They wouldn't dare bother their conscience with such trivial misdemeanours. Wouldn't condemn their own souls for a mere plank of wood.

There is singing outside on the streets.

Vespers is barely done and they are singing, drunken on the streets.

The singing gets closer.

Workmen. Drunk on their wages.

The singing is right outside the window. Nil looks down into the street.

They'll live like that for a year or two. Lose their jobs 'cause of it, nothing but vagrancy and petty theft left for them. So, the world shrinks.

Nil It's Perchikin.

Akulina appears in the kitchen doorway.

Akulina Father? Supper's ready.

Vassilly Perchikin . . .? Useless garbage.

Vassilly follows her out.

Elena It might be nicer upstairs. For tea.

Nil You don't want to stay down here?

Elena I don't know what I've done.

Pyotr It's his pride. He's very . . . A bit proud.

Nil A bit greedy. And a bit / evil.

Polya Shh. We don't need to –

Tanya Perhaps we just drop Father for now. You wouldn't want him to come back in the middle of it. Anyway, he's trying to be friendly. There hasn't been an argument for three days.

Pyotr Not for want of trying.

Tanya Drop it. He's old. We don't understand him. He doesn't understand us. We're all so. Harsh. Perhaps a bit of . . . kindness.

Nil While they sit on our face and tell us to eat our fill?

Pyotr would round on Nil, but Tanya just shakes her head in disgust. Vassilly returns in that gap. Everyone is clearly sitting on it.

Vassilly Pelegaya? Your father is drunk outside. Go and . . . move him on.

With a nod, Polya slips past Vassilly, followed by a swaggering Nil.

Yeah, you go too. Take a long look at your happy future. Well, it's all very quiet in here? Don't mind me.

Tanya We don't . . . it's normal.

Vassilly (*eyeing Elena*) You seem very. Cheery. Miss?

Pyotr How was the service?

Tanya Tea, Daddy? Or do you want your dinner?

Vassilly Tea, thanks.

Elena I'll pour it. Tanya, don't you –

Vassilly My daughter can pour it for me.

Pyotr Dad, I think. It doesn't matter. I think Elena was being –

Vassilly I didn't ask you. It's a principle. Tanya is my daughter. Elena is a stranger, an outsider. Nobody, to me. It's a principle. My daughter wanted to do something for me. This woman, whoever she might really be . . .? Has nothing to do with it.

Pyotr Father.

Tanya Pyotr.

Elena Don't.

Perchikin bursts in, drunk as a lord.

Perchikin Vassilly? Everyone? It's very important . . .

Vassilly Tea?

Perchikin Tea? No, no I've got / to talk.

Vassilly Vodka?

Teterev What's important?

Perchikin They've arrested Shyshkin and Tsvetaeva. /
The police.

Tanya What?

Nil returns to the room.

Perchikin The police. For inciting mutiny. Their play. / A
little play.

Tanya Shyshkin?

Elena (*simultaneously*) Inciting mutiny?

Pyotr (*simultaneously*) For their play?

Perchikin They've bundled them up. For questioning.
The police.

Pyotr What are you saying . . . ?

Nil Are you surprised?

Pyotr Am I what?

Perchikin So? You see? / Your friends.

Teterev Be *quiet*.

Perchikin I remembered the play. Weren't you all –?

Nil How did they find out about the play?

Tanya Why does that matter? Isn't that / what they do?

Nil It matters. Petya?

Pyotr Me?

Nil Well, it would help, wouldn't it?

Pyotr What?

Nil Clear your name. Get / your precious degree?

Pyotr What are you saying? / I haven't –

Nil Rent-collecting too slow?

Tanya Nil. Can you please –

Nil I just want to know. How they find out these things unless someone tells them?

Pyotr Your bloody soldiers tell them. / I said they –

Perchikin They're arrested too. It's all been during Vespers. The arrests. Rounding them up.

Nil That doesn't sound like a very good deal for the soldiers.

Pyotr Elena? Tanya? I don't, I didn't, I wouldn't. Why would I?

Nil You disgust / me.

Pyotr I disgust. What? I have not done this.

Elena Petya?

Pyotr What?

Elena You wouldn't . . . Petya. You.

Elena exits.

Pyotr Elena . . .?
No, no. This is not what I did.

Vassilly What does this mean? New lodgers?

Tanya Father. What kind of . . .?

Teterev That'd be convenient, wouldn't it? Vassilly?

Vassilly Polya, set the table.

Nil How can you eat?

Teterev Was that the plan?

Vassilly I don't have to answer to you.

Teterev Kill all those birds with *one stone*.

Vassilly I'm not going to defend *socialists*. In this house. My house.

Teterev Harbouring socialists, were you?
    Put the screws on you, did they?

Vassilly There's no screws on me.

Teterev And? What? You do a deal that keeps your family out of it?
    You didn't think they'd work it out?

Vassilly I know what I did. And I don't *need* to explain it. I certainly do not. To you.

Teterev It's not me I'm worried about.

    Quiet.

Vassilly I don't think any of you realise how it works. How the system works. And without it? What a mess.

Teterev So? When did you tell them? I had you pegged as a lame duck. But / you are poisonous.

Vassilly Tell them what?

Teterev You bark and bark and bark, but I didn't think you'd bite.

Vassilly Get out. All of you. GET OUT. THIS IS MY HOUSE.
    THIS IS MY HOUSE. AGAIN. MY FAMILY.

Pyotr Your family . . .?
    Well? Did you?

Vassilly This is a chance for you.

Pyotr To do what?

Vassilly What you want. What you said.

Yes, I told them. Yes. I did.

I don't have to. This is my house and what's not welcome here. *Is not* welcome here any longer. I've tolerated enough.

Nil What did you say? What did you think? You think this will be all right? You think you can make a deal with those people and not . . . Why? You think / that you'd get some kind of. *Revenge?*

Vassilly I didn't put you in it. I didn't put you in it. What's this? An interrogation?

Nil A conversation. Overdue conversation. Man to man.

Vassilly Nil? Can't you see? I brought / you up. RAISED YOU. UP.

Nil Don't you start with the *generosity.*

Polya grabs at Nil.

Polya You don't have to . . .

Vassilly Of course you don't. You wouldn't, because you are both as selfish as each other. Why else do you think my daughter is so sick?

Perchikin Vassilly. That's wrong.

Tanya Father, please. Don't use this. Please. Terenty? Pyotr? Someone stop this. It's not for this. Nil? Polya? *Go.* You should go . . . Please, please, please.

There is a senseless bustle spilling around Tanya, spinning and begging.

Polya Nil?

Nil Done, then. Pointless and noisy. Nothing new?

Vassilly Go, go. Take your bitch.

Nil Don't you –

Polya / Blaming me? For this?

Nil We are never. Never coming back.

Polya You shameless. People. To do. That.

Vassilly GET OUT.

Nil Exactly.

Perchikin Children? No. Gentle . . . some . . . No.

Polya Father? Come on.

Nil Now.

Perchikin No. I don't. No. Not like this, I won't leave like this. I didn't come for a war. My business here was to. No.

Teterev Come with me. Come with me.

Polya He'll just / throw you out.

Nil War is all there is here.

Perchikin No. I'll . . . Terenty? We can?

Pyotr (*to Nil*) Get out of here, quickly.

Nil I'm sorry.

Polya Let's go.

They leave. Silence.

Vassilly Is that how you leave? Is that how someone . . .

Pyotr Father, / you did this

Tanya / Please, let it.

Vassilly I'm trying to defend.
To. Stop. I didn't put Nil in it. I just . . .

Perchikin Better maybe to? Be quiet?

Vassilly It's so wrong. So wrong-way. Upside . . . (*To Perchikin*.) You fool, what did you / come here for today?

Tanya Father, please, no more?

Perchikin Vassilly. I'm stupid. I am. A fool. I just thought. I never thought. I just keep it simple. It's all you can do. One, two. A simple line of thought. Nothing more. In the end it's not up to us. See? And their politics, their politics? And their plays? They're only plays.

Vassilly Ohh . . . shut up.

Akulina pokes her head in from the kitchen.

Would he just. Leave like that? With no . . .

Teterev He has no choice. /
  What did you think?

Akulina What happened? I was in the larder. What's going on?

Vassilly Nil has left. For good.

Teterev Nil has been forced –

Akulina Good riddance.

Quiet.

Vassilly I'll see . . . I'll go and –

Pyotr No. Don't. You can't.

Tanya Daddy, really. Please?

Pyotr Think about it.

Vassilly This is my house.

Teterev / Not any more.

Pyotr Just. Stop picking at it.

Akulina What's going on?

Pyotr What have you done? Have you / any idea what –

Vassilly I AM DECIDING. It's very simple. I decide, see? I am the master of this house, regardless what you and your mob might think.

Perchikin Not at all, Vassilly. Everyone decides for themselves, can't you see? That's where you got off on the wrong –

Pyotr Where's Elena?

Teterev Packing her things.

Pyotr leaves to find her.

Vassilly Where are you going?
Answer me.

Teterev You have no authority left. This is what happens when you trade Evil for Good.

Vassilly Evil? You don't know the meaning of the word. Make your nest in our home and eat away and eat away at us. Tell him about the evil cuckoo, Perchikin.

Perchikin The cuckoo is a bird. He is a man.

Tanya Father look what you've done / to us.

Vassilly What I've done? I had no choice. To you? I had no choice. I had to defend you, both of you. All of us. I was defending what I've built. I had to choose. I made a decision.

Teterev You court destruction? You court the force of destruction and wonder why it destroys you?

Vassilly It hasn't destroyed anything. Nothing is destroyed. I've saved my home. So I lose rent from a few lodgers.

Pyotr and Elena appear.

Akulina Petya?

Pyotr I can't stay. I won't stay.

Akulina Petya, sweet.

Pyotr It's . . . It's too much.

Akulina No, no, no, no, no, no, no. NO.

Pyotr This is not what I did.

Vassilly What did you ever do? Who do you think you are? DO? What do you know about . . . ? You think this woman loves / you? You're not getting my money.

Pyotr This is the woman I love. This is the / woman . . .

Akulina How dare you? How dare you sink your claws into my son? You come in here with your ways. We know what you're about. / It's obvious what –

Elena I know what you're about.
    Holding. Grasping, drowning. You call it concern and love? You call it safety and well-being? All you want is to wring the life from them. Hold them under and keep them and control –

Vassilly They're young and stupid. I've spent fifty-eight years straining. Working for their. To have a future.

Pyotr What are you trying to say? Over and over again? That you've done . . . what? That I owe you? That I obey, like what? An employee? There are no more serfs. There is no more of this . . . what you think. What you imagine. Blind obedience. It's not like that any more.

Vassilly I'm trying to say . . .

Silence.

Teterev No. Really, go on.

Akulina Petya . . . Petya . . .

Tanya Mum. Please shut up.

Oh God. This is terrible. This is terrible. This is terrible. It's, it's, it's like a blunt saw. A blunt saw hacking at me. My soul. Over and over and over.

Silence.

Vassilly / Pyotr?

Elena Pyotr? This is. I've had enough. This is rubbish. / It's just stupid.

Pyotr Wait. For God's sake. Please?

Elena No. I can't do this any more, it's a nut-house.

Tanya It must be nearly over. Pyotr, please, you have to go.

Akulina Tanya . . . ?

Pyotr Everybody. Now listen. Mother. Father. Listen to me. This is the woman I love. And want. And, and want. And want to marry. Will. Marry.

Silence.

Teterev He should write. You should write. That was. Bang on.

Perchikin Fly away. Fly away from the cage.

Elena Let me go. I won't be. Used in this.

Pyotr No, please. It's not. I will make it clear. It will be.

Akulina You've destroyed yourself, Petya. Thrown yourself away.

Perchikin I don't know. What's Petya worth? Compared to her?

Teterev Well, there's a point.

Vassilly I mean. Good catch. You. You rubbed your . . . smeared your scent all over him second hand. Mangy. Cat.

Pyotr Father? You. No. You? NO.

Elena Oh yes. I took him, all right. I planned the whole thing and made all the moves. You hear me? I tore him away from you, from here. From this. Home? This lovely, happy home. You aren't people, you're a clinging. Rust. Some kind of dreadful.

Love? Love? This family is destroying him. I took him. And I hate you. Because I hate you.

Tanya Lena? Lena?

Pyotr Elena. Let's go.

Elena You know, I might not marry him. Yeah? Just for you? Just live with him, unmarried. Just fuck him. Just fuck him and fuck him and fuck him and never let him out of me. See? The plan? That's the plan. He will never leave me. You won't get near him to torment him. He won't come here and see you ever. And you know what I'll be doing? I will just be fucking him. All the time.

Teterev Wow.

Akulina Father? What . . . does . . . ?

Pyotr Elena. Let's.

They leave.

Perchikin Vassilly? She's not so bad. She's very cheery. She's –

Tanya Daddy, think / about . . .

Vassilly What are you doing here? You? You're the one should be married. It's all arse-about. It's all arse-about.

Perchikin Vassilly. Really. Look, look, think of it this way. Pyotr won't go back to university now? See? There's money in the bank.

He has something to live on. You've set a bit aside and she's. She's cheery and fun and lovely to look at. It looks better than you might think.

Vassilly rounds on Teterev.

Vassilly What's so funny? You? Get out too. Get out, all of you. The whole lot of you. Get out of my house.

Perchikin Vassilly?

Vassilly You too, you old . . . Useless, all of you. OUT.

Akulina Not you, Tanya, not you, darling. Don't worry, poor dear.

Tanya This . . . this. Why do so much damage on purpose? When all there is, all life does, all there ever is, *is* damage. Wouldn't you think? Wouldn't we try and do something else?

Vassilly You've hurt me. You've all . . . All you've ever thought about is yourself. No family. No love. / Nothing you care about.

Teterev Love? Did you say . . .

Vassilly Yes. Love. Home, family, you wouldn't understand.

Teterev I wouldn't go shouting that from the rooftops. I wouldn't go asking the punters to applaud this as a happy family.

Akulina Keep your opinions to yourself.

Teterev Impossible. Opinions hate being silent.

Perchikin Vassilly? You should look on the bright side of this. Your son's married and she's not a bad catch. Lot of / personality.

Vassilly Shut up.

Tanya Never mind.

Teterev Your son'll take after you.

Perchikin That's positive.

Teterev Not really. They are interchangeable.

Perchikin Father and son.

Teterev Mr Coward and Mr Stupid.

Perchikin Hang on. That's . . .

Vassilly Very funny.

Teterev He'll be as greedy as you. In his day, as mean and as harsh.
  He'll be as unhappy, as ungenerous, as unimaginative. Life will go on, people drop away, get left behind, sink into the oblivion of their inheritance . . . This is life. This is what you made.

Vassilly Very. Funny. Shut these people up and get out. I am not some . . . I'm not the idiot you think. You, too. Have. Both of you. All of you. You. You have hurt me too.

Teterev Not enough. I wish I could take more credit.

Perchikin Come. Let's . . .

Perchikin takes Teterev away. Silence.

Vassilly Mother. Mother . . .

Akulina and Vassilly go to the kitchen. Only Tanya remains.

Tanya That's not. I didn't want . . .

Tanya slumps to the piano and the dissonant chords fill the air.

End.